T4-AJR-568

OUTLINES OF MISSIONARY HISTORY

ALFRED DeWITT MASON

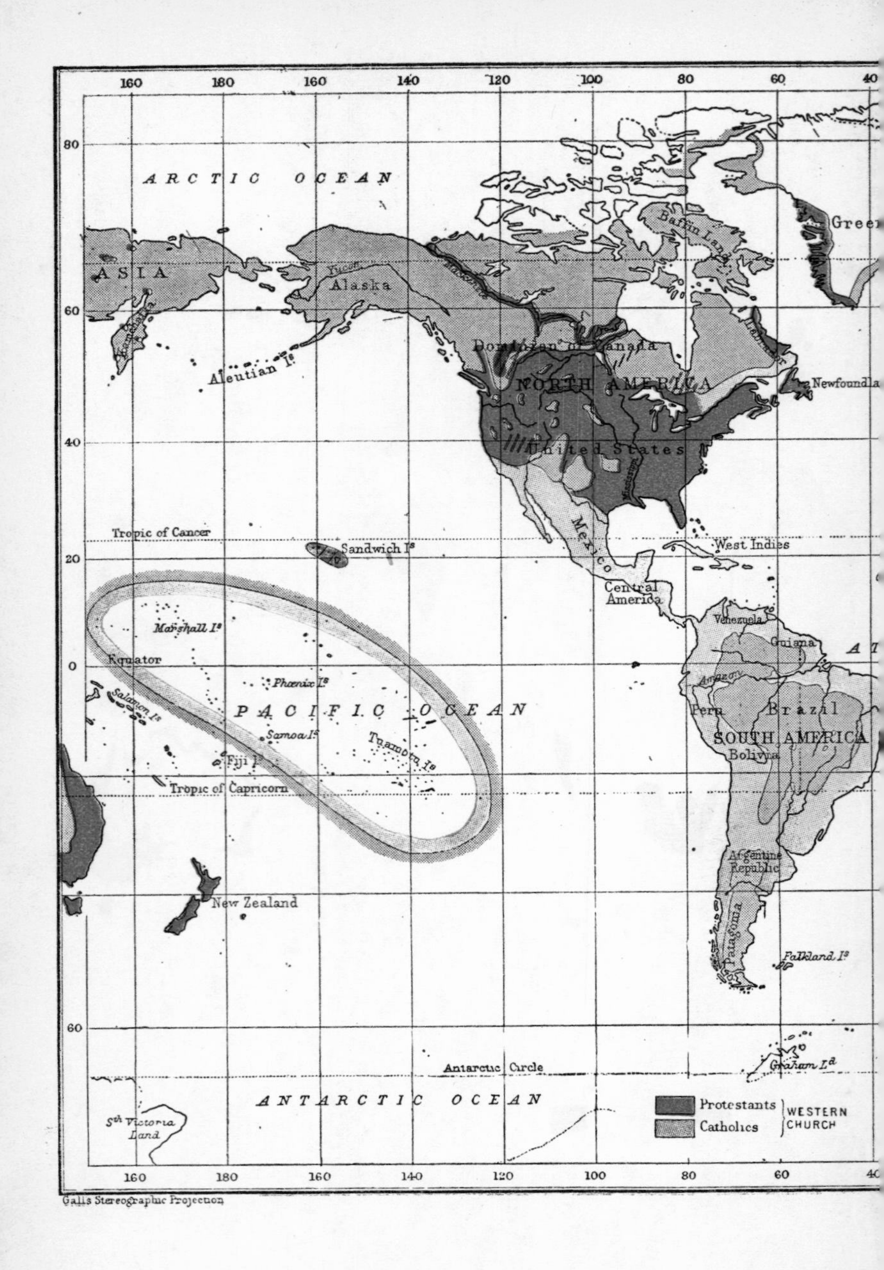

Gall's Stereographic Projection

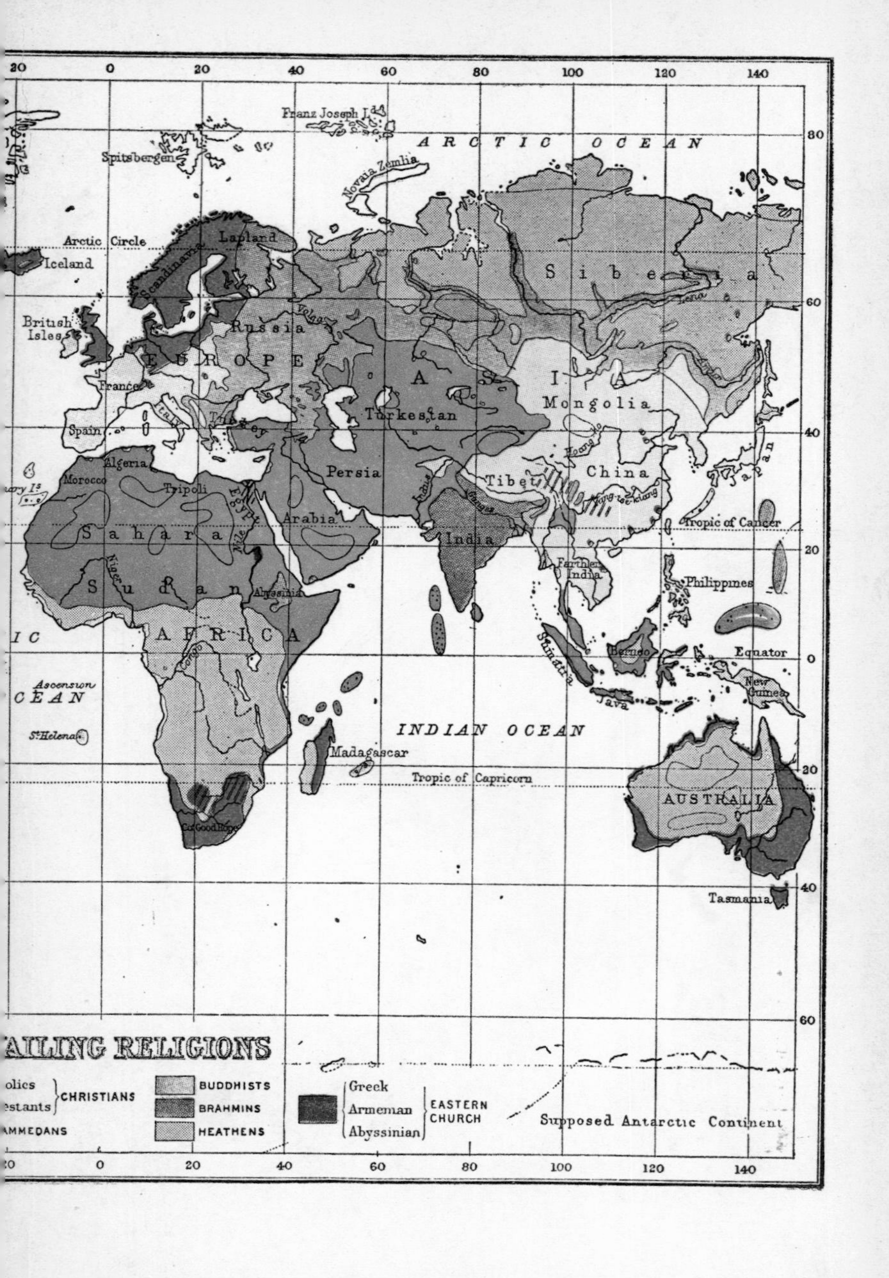

AILING RELIGIONS
olics
estants
CHRISTIANS
AMMEDANS
BUDDHISTS
BRAHMINS
HEATHENS
Greek
Armenian
Abyssinian
EASTERN CHURCH
ARCTIC OCEAN
INDIAN OCEAN
Franz Joseph Ld.
Spitsbergen
Novaia Zemlia
Arctic Circle
Iceland
Lapland
Scandinavia
British Isles
Russia
EUROPE
France
Spain
Italy
Turkey
Siberia
ASIA
Mongolia
Turkestan
Persia
Arabia
Tibet
China
India
Farther India
Japan
Tropic of Cancer
Philippines
Borneo
Sumatra
Java
New Guinea
Equator
Algeria
Morocco
Tripoli
Egypt
Sahara
Sudan
Abyssinia
AFRICA
Congo
Niger
Nile
Ascension
St. Helena
Madagascar
Tropic of Capricorn
C. of Good Hope
AUSTRALIA
Tasmania
Supposed Antarctic Continent
Volga
Lena
Indus
Ganges
Hoang-ho
Yang-tse-kiang

Outlines of Missionary History

By

ALFRED DEWITT MASON, D. D.

LECTURER ON THE HISTORY OF MISSIONS IN THE
UNION MISSIONARY TRAINING INSTITUTE,
BROOKLYN, NEW YORK.

Revised Edition with Maps

NEW YORK
GEORGE H. DORAN COMPANY

Revised and Corrected, 1921

PRINTED IN THE UNITED STATES OF AMERICA

TO MY WIFE,

ELIZABETH SWAIN MASON,

WHOSE ZEAL AND FAITH HAVE INSPIRED MANY TO LABOR FOR THE EXTENSION OF GOD'S KINGDOM, THIS BOOK IS AFFECTIONATELY DEDICATED.

INTRODUCTION

The voices that are coming out of the East with increasing frequency in these days are being listened to more than formerly and with distinct advantage to ourselves. They not only interpret to us the life and thought of other peoples, but they convey to us the careful observations of those who have gone out from amongst us upon the errands of God and of the Church and who have cast in their lot with those people. One of these latter has recently sent out with peculiar force an appeal to which this book is a distinct and somewhat unique response.

The thought that thus comes to us and which should be given heed to with especial care at this time, is that, if the evangelization of the world is a truer conception of the duty of the Church than mere proselytism for its own sake, the conception of the Church's responsibility must deepen into something very much more than mere interest in foreign missions, and her efforts must be something more than the purely superficial attempts to keep up that interest by the spectacular attractions and displays which may momentarily arrest the eye, but can not so assuredly and permanently affect the heart. If missionary work has to depend upon the power of keeping up such an interest its day is past. It is not interest alone, but passion—the passion that comes from full knowledge, deep living and high thinking that the Church needs.

There is, of course, a right place for these things. But while the interest of the child is childlike, the mere interest of the adult is childish. Let us have interest in the Sunday school, but let us have passion in the Church, based upon some knowledge of its progress. We must expect from the Church more than interest in that work of redemption for which Christ endured the agony of a Gethsemane and the heartbreak of a Calvary. The Master went to His death amidst apparent failure and defeat, content to foresee the result of that travail of His soul which should satisfy. The work which was thus initiated by the passion of Christ can hardly be carried on only as it appeals to the interest of the Church.

This book, which so well attains the object that the author sets himself, of presenting an outline of missionary history from the earliest times, covering all the so-called missionary continents and islands, and including within its wide scope that same missionary work of the Church which is carried on at home is, in my judgment, a very distinct contribution to missionary literature in general, and in particular to the meeting of this special appeal that comes out of the mission field.

There is another impression which a perusal of it can not but leave upon the mind of the reader. Ample illustration is afforded of the truth of Prof. Lindsay's profound observation:

"History knows nothing of revivals of moral living apart from some new religious impulse. The motive power needed has always come through leaders who have had communion with the Unseen." One, therefore, reads again with peculiar satisfaction, in the pages of this book, that in the great advances of the Christian Church God has raised up continually as leaders those "that do know their God" and have thus accomplished "exploits" in His name.

By reason of the emphasis which the developments of recent decades have placed upon the Far East, conspicuous names connected with those lands are more familiar to us. But it is with some surprise and with deep interest that one is both reminded and informed of the splendid leadership which has been afforded to the Church in the history of its early progress in Europe, and of its later remarkable achievements in Africa and the Islands of the Sea. Thus the oft-repeated statement that missionary biography is one of the most fruitful means of deepening and making more abiding the interest in the missionary operations of the Church is again strikingly illustrated in this book.

It is with peculiar pleasure that I find myself associated in this very limited way with the author in the admirable purpose that lies behind this book and which he has carried out with so much success.

William I. Chamberlain,

Corresponding Secretary, Board of Foreign Missions of the Reformed Church in America.

PREFACE

THIS book has grown out of a necessity. For some years past it has been the annual privilege of the writer to conduct a class of students through a short course in the History of Missions. His endeavor has been to acquaint them sufficiently with the topic to induce a further interest in it without burdening the memory with a mass of dates, names and incidents which might soon be forgotten. A text-book along these lines does not seem to be at present attainable. In this book the attempt has been made to so combine a reasonable fullness of detail with some vividness of description and with the personal touch which accompanies a biographical treatment of the topic, that not only the student but the general reader may be led to pursue the subject further as time and opportunity may permit.

Grateful acknowledgment is made to the Rev. William I. Chamberlain, Ph. D., D. D., the Corresponding Secretary of the Board of Foreign Missions of the Reformed Church in America, for his introductory word and his many helpful suggestions, and to the numerous authorities to whom reference has been made and whose words, in many instances, have been quoted in full so that they may thus give personal expression to their statements and views.

If what has now been written shall conduce in any degree to awaken or deepen the reader's interest in the "wonderful works" which through His messengers Christ has wrought among the nations of the earth, the purpose of this book will have been attained.

A. DeW. M.

Brooklyn, N. Y., March, 1912.

Note to Third Edition

The adoption of these "Outlines" as a textbook by many missionary schools and training classes having created a steady demand for it, a revised edition was published in November, 1915, and now another edition is called for.

Advantage has therefore been taken of this opportunity to revise some portions of the book and to add to it a chapter (XVIII) on "The Effect of the World War upon Missions." A set of questions has also been provided for the use of leaders who may desire them; the bibliography and statistics revised and a new, and it is believed, an original feature added in a series of charts showing the Expansion of Christianity.

With these revisions and additions this book is again sent forth with a prayer of thanksgiving for its past usefulness and of petition for its continued usefulness in the future.

A. DeW. M.

October, 1921.

CONTENTS

MAPS AND CHARTS

Outlines of Missionary History

CHAPTER I

INTRODUCTORY

The History of Christian Missions is a topic of wide scope and large importance. It has to do with the motives and the deeds of those who, from the time of the Great Commission to the present day, have gone up and down the highways and the byways of earth proclaiming to all men, [1]"The Kingdom of heaven is at hand; repent ye and believe the gospel." It is one of the great departments of the records of human thought and interests, and some knowledge of it is therefore essential not only to the student, but as well to the man of affairs who is interested in the origin and development of the greatest enterprise that has ever engaged the thought or action of mankind.

At the very beginning of such a study it is necessary to have some clear and brief definition of our topic, and the one that is suggested in the answer to the natural query, "What is Christian missions?" is this, "Christian missions is the proclamation of the gospel to the unconverted according to the command of Christ."

Let us dwell a moment on the important words of this definition.

[1] Mark 1:15.

The root idea of the word "mission" or "missions" is to send (Latin, *mitto*). The missionary is, therefore, one who is sent. He is simply a messenger. He goes not at his own initiative, nor to accomplish a purpose which he has originated, but as the agent of the one who sends him and to do that for which he is commissioned; and the more absolutely he succeeds in simply representing the One who has sent him, and the more intelligently, faithfully and consecratedly he does his work, the more perfectly does he fulfill his mission.

Another word of importance in this definition is "proclamation," which literally means "to shout out" a thing. And that is the fundamental thought of the missionary message. We are to "cry aloud and spare not." Our word is one of warning as well as of good news—"Except ye repent, ye shall all likewise perish," and who would think of ever sounding an alarm in a gentle whisper or with soothing accents?

The message thus proclaimed is "the gospel," the good news, the message of which Christ Himself was the first messenger, [2]"God so loved the world that He gave His only begotten Son that whosoever believeth in Him should not perish, but have everlasting life;" [3]"The Son of man is come to seek and to save that which was lost." This "good news" includes all the blessings that accompany and flow from the gospel. Civilization,

[2] John 3:16. [3] Luke 19:20.

good order, progress, peace, humanity, liberty of life and thought and speech,—all that men deem worth living for, is the fruit of the gospel.

Another vital term of this definition is "the unconverted," signifying those either who through ignorance do not know or through willfulness or indifference neglect or reject the gospel. These are sometimes called "heathen," sometimes "pagan," sometimes "unbelievers," sometimes "non-Christian," but all are comprehended in the word "unconverted,"—not turned to Christ. They are like those to whom the prophet cried, [4]"Turn ye, turn ye, for why will ye die, O house of Israel," and those others to whom the Saviour Himself said in sorrow, [5]"Ye will not come unto Me that ye might have life."

These unconverted are found everywhere. Darkest Africa hides no sadder cases of sinful rejection of the Christ than does enlightened America. We talk about foreign missions, or home missions, or city missions; but all these terms are simply convenient designations of relative situation, and no discrimination as to their worth or need, such as is often thoughtlessly made, should ever be expressed. In each case, and whether the sinner is such through excusable ignorance or inexcusable willfulness, the danger is the same, and the remedy is one, even as the drowning man must be rescued from his peril, whether his danger has arisen from a reckless disregard or an

[4]Ezek. 33:11. [5]John 5:40.

utter ignorance of the power of the mighty tide that is dragging him down to death.

Finally, in our definition, we must recognize that the only right we have to go as messengers to the unconverted with the gospel of salvation through Christ is the fact that He has commanded us to do so. [6]"Go ye, therefore, and disciple all nations" is not a polite request, not the mere expression of a wish, not a simple suggestion; but a short, sharp, direct, explicit, peremptory and permanent order from the Great Captain of our salvation to us, His soldiers, "Go." To be obedient and faithful to Him, we must go in person or by substitute, with direct or indirect appeal, through our influence or by our gifts, and wherever we can reach the unconverted we must bring to them the one supreme message, [7]"The Kingdom of heaven is at hand, repent ye and believe the gospel."

[8]"Go ye into all the world and preach the gospel to every creature" was the final, the most imperative and the most inclusive command of the risen Christ. In it the Christian Church of every age should perceive her universal message and her most important duty.

After the question, "What is meant by Christian missions?" the next query naturally is, "What are the essential qualifications of the missionary?" "What must be the spirit of him who would carry to his fellow-men this message of salvation?" The answer to this is threefold:

[6] Matt. 28:19. [7] Mark 1:15. [8] Mark 16:15.

1. He must have the spirit of *Obedience.* The basis of his work is the command of Christ, and to make that command an actuality, the spirit of obedience to it must be the great foundation principle of the missionary's life. [9]"Ye have not chosen Me, but I have chosen you and ordained you, that ye should go and bring forth fruit," were Christ's words to His early disciples, and the fact remains the same to-day. The missionary does not go from his own free choice in the human sense,—an obligation is laid upon his soul, and with Paul he exclaims, [10]"Woe is me if I preach not the gospel." Thus driven by this inward sense of need, he goes forth to conquer the world for Christ, or to die in the attempt, his face toward the foe.

2. And he must also have the spirit of *Love.* Obedience may compel, but love will sustain him. [11]"Greater love hath no man than this, that a man lay down his life for his friends. Ye are My friends, if ye do whatsoever I have commanded you." Obedience may be the foundation of the Christian's work, but love is the fair superstructure which rises beautiful and enduring upon the rock of faith-filled obedience to the Master's Word.

3. But even obedience and love will not wholly fit the man for his work. He may add to these the qualities of an educated mind, a refined and consecrated intellect, a persuasive manner and the knowledge and use of the best methods of work,

---

[9] John 15:16. [10] I. Cor. 9:16. [11] John 15:13, 14

and yet even all these are not wholly sufficient. One essential quality must be had—*Power,* that power which only the Holy Spirit can impart and without which the best meant efforts will be barren of results. The promise of Christ to His disciples was and still is, [12]"Ye shall receive *power* after the Holy Ghost is come upon you," and then, and only then, can they be "witnesses" who shall testify with convicting and convincing force to the mercy of God in Christ Jesus, and to the love of that Saviour who came into the world that the world through Him might be saved.

One other important question remains to be answered, "What have been and what are the principal motives which have influenced the Christian Church in the establishment and maintenance of missionary work?"

Five may be mentioned, of which the first is: The exaltation of Jesus Christ. This was probably one of the first and strongest motives in the early Church. Jesus Christ, through the preaching of the gospel by the apostles and their successors, had claimed the allegiance of the world as their Saviour. But His claim was not only disputed, but ridiculed. He was [13]"despised" as well as rejected of men. He was regarded as simply a condemned criminal, an offender against the Jewish law, who had been executed for the dreadful crime of blasphemy; or at best He was looked upon as [14]"beside Himself" with fanati-

[12] Acts 1:8. [13] Isa. 53:3. [14] Mark 3:21.

cism and ambition. His divinity was neither accepted nor understood. His doctrines of love and mercy seemed a confession of weakness. His humility was translated into fear or cowardice. In a word, Jesus Christ was considered as either a keen impostor or a harmful enthusiast and treated accordingly by the wise and the mighty of His day. It was, therefore, the first duty and the first effort of His disciples to show His true nature, the justice of His claims, the righteousness of His demands, the beauty and holiness of His character, and the divinity of His person and His work. To this all their efforts and all their preaching were directed, and so effectually that before three hundred years had elapsed after His birth the Roman world, which had so despised and slandered Jesus of Nazareth, was, in form at least, acknowledging Him as the Christ of God. And the same motive must still be potent, because there are still many in the world who in reality, if not by outward act, despise Jesus as greatly as did those enemies who delivered Him to Pontius Pilate. In Japan, not sixty years ago, the religion of Jesus was forbidden as a pestilential thing, and the Christian converts, if found, were compelled to trample on the cross. In many other lands to-day Christianity is despised, and even in nominally Christian countries thousands and millions are to be found who, by their attitude of contempt and hatred, [15]"crucify the Son of God

[15] Heb. 6:6.

afresh and put Him to an open shame." It must still, therefore, be a strong motive of the Christian missionary, whether at home or abroad, to exalt Jesus, to show the loveliness of His character, the greatness of His mercy, the terribleness of His wrath, and the dignity and honor of His crown and throne.

A second motive prominent in the history of missions is the desire for the salvation of men. This possibly takes precedence even of the first motive, and perhaps always has, for if any one is converted to Christ and his salvation has been thus secured, his honor and reverence for the Lord Jesus is of course assured. And to him who realizes the truth of the declaration, [16]"Neither is there salvation in any other, for there is none other name under heaven given among men whereby we must be saved," this motive will surely be all powerful. It follows the course of a natural impulse. Men are in danger of eternal death. Without the knowledge of Christ as a Saviour they are lost. There is, then, but one supreme duty for the disciples of Christ, to go to every man with the message of salvation and to beseech them in [17]"Christ's name to be reconciled to God."

A third motive is the uplift or betterment of our fellow-men. There are those to whom even the material benefits of Christianity appear great enough to warrant the work of missions amid un-

[16] Acts 4:12. [17] 2 Cor. 5:20.

civilized peoples. The writer was once told by one who had been for years a very earnest and consecrated missionary in India, that he would consider his life and strength well spent if only he were able to lift up the common people of India to the enjoyment of some of the intellectual and material benefits of modern civilization. But it would seem as if this motive were hardly sufficient. We can not forget the divine word, [18]"Seek ye first the Kingdom of God and His righteousness, and all these things shall be *added* unto you." Nevertheless it is true that we must consider that the material advantages of Christianity are in themselves very great, and that when *added* to spiritual blessings they are of inestimable value, even great enough to warrant one in giving much attention to them. We need but to recall the examples of Livingstone in his antagonism to the African slave trade; of Mackay, of Uganda, in his training of the natives in the mechanical arts; of Dr. Parker, who opened the way for the gospel in China by his medical work, and of Dr. Verbeck's educational work in Japan, to realize that the material gifts of Christianity to lands that have less of temporal blessings than have Christian nations, have been wonderful in their ultimate influence upon the spiritual life of such peoples.

In the missionary work of the Christians of the period of the Middle Ages, we find another strong

---

[18] Matt. 6:33.

motive arising from the gradual centralizing of Christian life and activity in the Church of Rome and from the conviction that the Church's rule to be effective must be material and direct and coequal, if not superior, in its authority to that of the State. Thus the motive of the supremacy of the visible Church and the extension of its rule, both as a spiritual and in many ways as a governmental power, took possession of the minds of the Christian Church, and for many centuries that motive dominated her relations to all those peoples with whom she came into contact.

A last motive that has had great influence over the Church in her times of greatest power, has been the desire for the conquest of the world for Christ. Christ is our King, mankind His rightful subjects; all who knowingly reject His rule are, therefore, rebels against the highest authority in heaven or on earth, and the Church, as the expression of Christ's will on earth, must be His instrument in making known that will to all men, thus hastening the day [19]"when every knee shall bow and every tongue confess that Jesus Christ is Lord to the glory of God the Father." It is no temporal rule that is thus proposed or sought, and in this respect it differs absolutely and essentially from the motive of the domination of the Church as a temporal power. It is rather a spiritual rule such as was voiced in the warcry of the Cromwellians in England, "For

[19] Phil. 2:10.

Christ's Crown and Covenant,'' whereby not through external conformity alone, but through spiritual agreement with the will of God, there shall be realized on earth the vision of that heavenly condition in which all men shall acknowledge that [20]''One is their Master, even Christ, and all they are brethren.''

These five motives then, viz.: The exaltation of Christ as Lord; the salvation of the souls of men; the uplift of men by bettering their physical and moral condition; the elevation of the Church to the place of supreme control in the State, and the extension of the Kingdom of God over all the earth, have been for the most part the controlling influences in the establishment and development of the great missionary enterprises of the Christian Church from the time of her founding until the present day.

Matt. 23:8.

CHAPTER II

APOSTOLIC MISSIONS

THE history of missions may be divided into six periods, of which the first period, extending from the death of Christ to the death of John (33-100 A. D.) is called the Period of Apostolic Missions. This period began with the earthly ministry of our Lord. His life for more than three years was that of the itinerant missionary. Up and down through the land of Palestine He went [1]"teaching in their synagogues and preaching the gospel of the Kingdom and healing every sickness and all manner of disease among the people." He had His missionary training class, His spiritual clinic, in which He not only taught His disciples the principles of the gospel which was to form the subject of His scholars' work, but by manifold examples explained His teaching and enforced His wonderful words by His equally wonderful works of mercy and compassion. And when the Lord's earthly work was brought to a close and the twelve leaders of the newly born Church had received the enduement of the Holy Spirit, immediately the great missionary work of the Church began, and the Apostolic Period of Christian Missions was fully inaugurated.

We must not, however, think of the apostles

[1] Matt. 4:23.

as the only missionaries of this period, nor of their work as the only important or even the most important missionary enterprise then carried on. This work was done by a multitude of Christians, for, as we read, [2]"they that were scattered abroad," by the persecution that arose after the martyrdom of Stephen, "went everywhere preaching the Word." It was therefore a time of individual effort, of general consecration to the work of proclaiming the gospel; in a word, it was not a movement of the leaders, but of the common people, the "laymen's missionary movement" of the first century. [3]"There was no widely extended missionary organization; there was scarcely even a Church as we understand that term. There was simply a constantly increasing number of individual believers who, wherever they went, whether on their regular business or driven by persecution, preached Christ, told the story of the Cross, bore witness to its value for themselves, and urged the acceptance of the Saviour on those with whom they came in contact. Of missionaries in the modern sense of the term there were not many; of those who devoted their full time and strength to the work of preaching there were very few, but of those who made their trade, their profession, their everyday occupation, of whatever nature it was, the means of extending their faith, there was a multitude."

Acts 8:4. [3] "The Missionary Enterprise," p. 14.

And this method of the gospel propaganda was wonderfully efficient. Even so early in the history of the Church as the Day of Pentecost, only forty days after Jesus' ascension, the list of the representatives of various nations, who, as visitors to Jerusalem, had heard the gospel message, is astonishingly large. And in a few years Paul is writing to the chief cities of Asia Minor and of Greece, and even to Rome itself, instructing, admonishing, and cheering the missionary Churches that had been established in these influential national centers.

Thus the apostolic period, though the most brief of all the divisions of the missionary work of the Church, was perhaps more fruitful than any period that has succeeded it, nor is it likely that at any time during the Church's history has her missionary work so completely absorbed her attention and effort. It was the well-nigh universal occupation of the Church of the first century, and with such vigor and faith was the work pursued that ere the last apostle, whose sorrow-darkened eyes had seen his Master hanging on the cross of Calvary, had been translated to the glories of that heaven which the Master had promised His disciples, there were but few important districts of the great Roman world that had not at least heard of this new faith.

It must not be thought, however, that this growth was attained without the severest opposition. The execution of Stephen and the persecutions led by Saul were but the forerunners of a long and pitiless attempt to root out this "pestilent superstition." Nations and rulers who were the natural enemies of each other united in their opposition to the faith of the Crucified One, and their attempts to quench the ardor of His friends gave rise to many periods when the struggling Church seemed to have almost succumbed to the fury of their oppressors. But after each baptism of fire the friends of Christ rose undismayed and boldly testified to His name in the very face of their relentless foes.

Let us learn, by but one example, how these early Christians testified for Christ. Polycarp, who was martyred about 165 A. D., is reputed to have been the pupil of the Apostle John and to have been ordained by the apostle himself as bishop or minister of the Church at Smyrna. But neither his reputation for holiness, nor the beauty of his character, nor the usefulness of a life spent in charity and good works could save him from the fury of the enemies of Christ, and during the great persecution of the Church which took place in the reign of the Emperor Marcus Aurelius (165 A. D.) Polycarp was arrested and brought before the Roman proconsul to answer for his life. "Blaspheme Christ," cried the proconsul, willing to spare the venerable man who stood before him, "Blaspheme Christ and you shall be freed." But, standing before the vast multitude of fanatical spectators, thirsting for his blood, the aged Christian with unshaken voice made answer: "Eighty and six years have I served my Lord Christ and He has never done me wrong. How can I then blaspheme my King who has saved me?" and bound to the fatal stake, with the flames leaping around him, Polycarp passed to his reward in a chariot of fire.

No wonder that with such witnesses for Christ during the ten great persecutions which ravaged the early Church, beginning with that of Nero, in A. D. 64, and ending with the Diocletian persecution in 303, the Church not only lived, but grew and waxed strong, thus proving the truth of the familiar saying, "The blood of the martyrs is the seed of the Church." Indeed, so far and fast had the cause of Christ spread and such firm hold had it taken upon the diverse peoples of the Roman Empire, in spite of the opposition of philosopher and emperor, that as early as the close of the second century Tertullian could say to the heathen of Africa, "We are but of yesterday, and yet we already fill your cities, islands, camps, your palaces, senate, and forum; we have left you only your temples;" and even half a century earlier Justin Martyr, himself a contemporary of the later apostles, declared: "There is no people, Greek or barbarian or of any other race, by whatsoever appellation or manner they may be distinguished, however ignorant of arts or of agriculture, whether they dwell in tents or wander about in covered wagons, among whom prayers and thanksgivings are not offered in the name of the crucified Jesus to the Father and Creator of all things."

At last the natural consummation of so wonderful a development was reached, and in A. D. 313, by the imperial edict of Constantine, Christianity was recognized as the official religion of the Roman world and took its place in history as a great world religion. Such was the marvelous change in three centuries from the faith of slaves to that of kings. No wonder has it been related that Julian the Apostate, viewing the triumphs of the cross, exclaimed, "O Galilean, Thou hast conquered!"

And yet, this seeming triumph of the faith marked in a sense the beginning of a period of less energetic effort in its propagation. Exalted upon the throne of the Cæsars, the Christian Church began to think that its long struggle for recognition was happily ended. The fervor of its first love, the energy of its early efforts began to slacken. The dangers and foes also which at first had threatened it from without began to attack it from within. The [4]"perilous times" of which Paul warned the Church very soon began to manifest themselves, and though the wind of persecution and material opposition died away, the enervating sunshine of governmental protection and popularity threatened to do more evil than the severest storm-blasts had accomplished. The

[4] 2 Tim. 3:1.

purity and simplicity of the early faith began to abate and heresies and crudities of thought to arise within the Church itself. Thus the battle of the Church was no longer waged alone with heathenism without, but also with heathenism within, and the great Patristic controversies that lasted for many years diverted the attention of the Church from the task of propagating the gospel to that of defining and defending the faith once delivered to the saints.

CHAPTER III

PATRISTIC OR EARLY CHURCH MISSIONS

Thus it came to pass during the second period of the history of missions, which is called the Period of the Early Church or the Patristic Period (100-800), that battles for the faith at home and labors for the propagation of the truth abroad divided the attention of the Church. This condition developed two widely differing classes of Christian champions, the one of which contended against the philosophies of the non-Christian thinkers and the false doctrines which sprang quickly up among the professed friends of Christ; and the others, leaving such contests to the Church at home, and to such mighty apologists and theologians as Athanasius, Jerome, Chrysostom, Augustine, and others, fared forth to distant lands and unfamiliar peoples to plant the faith in which they themselves trusted. Among these missionaries of the early Church we first note Ulfilas, or Wulfila, which means "Little Wolf." He was born 311 A. D., and came from Christian parents who had been captured and enslaved during one of the many incursions made by the Goths into Asia Minor about the middle of the third century. His family were people of rank and influence, as is indicated by the fact that as a young man he was taken in an embassy sent by Alaric, king of the Goths, to Constantinople, where he remained for ten years. He then returned as a missionary to his own people (341) and labored among the Goths north of the Danube River. His particular distinction comes from the fact that he [1]"was one of the first missionaries to give not only Christianity but letters to a whole people. The Goths were without books or writing. In order that they might have the Scriptures, Ulfilas invented for them an alphabet, using a modification of the Greek letters with the addition of some characters to represent Gothic sounds for which the Greeks had no signs. He translated the whole Bible, except the Books of Kings, omitting these because he feared that they would tend to feed the warlike passions of the Goths. Only his translation of the New Testament, however, has come down to us, the best extant copy of which is now in the University of Upsala, Sweden. It is known as the "silver Bible" because the letters are written with silver ink upon a purple background. It is extremely precious to the world because it is the earliest existing form of the Teutonic speech, the mother language of all Northern Europe and America."

An early missionary to the Gauls, who left the most permanent impress on the inhabitants of the land that we now know as France, was

---

1 "Two Thousand Years Before Carey," p. 294.

Martin, Bishop of Tours (316-400). He did not introduce Christianity among the Franks, as many, including such noted men as Irenæus and Pothinus and Benignus, friends and disciples of Polycarp, had long before carried the gospel to these savage tribes. But his character and work were such that he finally established Christianity over a wide area of Gaul where it had been hitherto but imperfectly known or received. He was a soldier under Constantine before he became a Christian, which no doubt accounts for the manner in which he waged war against heathenism, organizing his monks into a sort of army, not, however, to fight with men, but to cut down sacred trees, destroy idols and temples, and thus to remove the traces of paganism from those communities which his preaching and instruction had led to embrace Christianity. For centuries Martin of Tours has been the patron saint of France. St. Martin's day is noted in the Scottish civil calendar as "Martinmas," and in Germany and France it is observed as a feast day. In early days the tomb of St. Martin was a shrine, and his motto, "*Non recuso laborem*" (I will not draw back from the work), became a watchword for missionaries in all Western Europe.

It certainly is somewhat strange that the name which popularly stands for that of the typical Irishman was not the name of any Irishman at all, but of a Scotchman, whose zeal for Christianity led him to brave captivity and toils that he might plant the banner of the cross amid the wild tribesmen of ancient Erin. Succat, or Patricius (to use the Latin form of the name, from which we get our familiar name Patrick), was born in Dumbartonshire, Scotland, near the present city of Glasgow, in the latter part of the fifth century (493). When about sixteen years old he was taken captive by a raiding party from Ireland and sold as a slave to a chieftain named Milcho, living in what is now County Antrim, who made him his shepherd and cowboy. Patrick's father was a deacon or priest in Scotland, and the youth was well instructed in Christianity, while his religious life was maintained by much prayer and meditation, for which his solitary occupation gave him frequent opportunities. After a while he escaped and returned to Gaul, and there remained some years, possibly coming under the influence of the monastic school of Martin of Tours, in France, which was at that time a flaming center of missionary zeal. Returning to Scotland, he had a vision much like that of Paul's vision of the man of Macedonia, dreaming that he saw a man from Ireland who gave him a letter headed "The Voice of the Irish," and that he heard the voices of men who dwelt near where he had been held captive crying out, "We entreat thee, holy youth, to come and walk still among us." Obedient to this heavenly vision, Patrick left his native land and landed at Wicklow, but was driven away from there. Sailing north, he entered Strangford

Lough, in County Down, and in a barn near where is now Downpatrick, the first Christian Church in Ireland was gathered. Beginning about the year 525, he "did the work of an evangelist" with rare zeal and discretion, founding churches, schools, and monasteries, and preaching the gospel throughout the length and breadth of that wild and savage land.

He was God's instrument to establish Christianity in Ireland, but that he was a member of the Romish Church, as we understand it, is not historical. [2]"The authentic records do not indicate that Patrick had any connection with the pope or with popery. The modern Romish sect did not then exist. Patrick's grandfather was a married priest. There is no auricular confession, no adoration of Mary, no extreme unction in the reliable records of his life. The most striking feature in his own writings is the frequent citation of Scripture, which he quotes from the version translated by Jerome. This, with a life of Martin of Tours, is bound up with the 'Book of Armagh,' which is the title of the collection of St. Patrick's extant writings. It is forever significant that the life of a preceding missionary and a copy of the New Testament should be bound up with the primitive account of the first distinguished missionary to the British Islands."

If Ireland was evangelized by a Scotchman, Scotland was later repaid for her gift by the

2 "Two Thousand Years Before Carey," p. 265.

labors among her people of the eminent Irish missionary Columba. He was of royal lineage, from one of the numerous families of Celtic chieftains, and was born about 521. Having studied for the Church, he was early distinguished for his piety and zeal, and laid the foundations of several monastic communities while he was yet a young man.

When forty-two years old (563)) he crossed the Irish Channel to Argyllshire, Scotland, and with twelve companions founded, on the little island of Hii or Iona, a settlement which became one of the most famous missionary schools in history. From this school went forth many to spread the gospel tidings throughout Scotland, and, as says a writer, [3]"for two centuries or more Iona was the place in all the world whence the greatest amount of evangelistic influence went forth and on which, therefore, the greatest amount of blessing from on high rested." The extent of his work and that of the "graduates" of his "missionary training school," is indicated by the fact that, "during Columba's lifetime the gospel was generally accepted by the whole of the Western Picts; by the population of the Hebrides, whose numbers were probably but small, but among whom missionary work must have been carried on with immense difficulty; and by many in the Orkney, Shetland, and Faroe Islands."

Turning from Scotland to England, we note that the great pioneer missionary to this land was

---

[3] "Medieval Missions," pp. 50, 51.

Augustine, who, with his band of forty Benedictine monks, was sent by Pope Gregory to re-evangelize a people whose ancestors had once been evangelized but later had relapsed into heathenism through the weakness of the Church and the growing influence of pagan tribes. Augustine and his helpers seem to have been dismayed at first by the reports of the savage character of the Saxons and to have turned back, seeking to be released from their dangerous mission. But Gregory, who long before he became pope had determined on the evangelization of the people of the fair-haired slaves whom he saw in the market-place at Rome, sent back his agents with the stern command to persevere in their work. Pressing on, therefore, this early missionary deputation, in the year 596, came to the kingdom of Kent, whose ruler, Ethelbert, had married a wife of the Franks, Bertha by name, who was herself a Christian. Influenced by her, Ethelbert received the strangers with kindness, assigned them a residence in his capital city of Canterbury, and gave them permission to preach and to teach any who would hear them. So well did they succeed that within a year after the landing of the missionaries, Ethelbert was baptized and, according to the method of the times, the nation followed their ruler in the acceptance of the new faith. The Church of St. Martin, in Canterbury, is still pointed out as the site whereon Christianity was re-established in Britain.

Germany, inhabited by rude tribes whose

earlier civilization and Christianity had been almost wholly obliterated by the waves of barbaric invasion from the North and East that swept over it during the second and third centuries, was resown with the gospel seed, not, as would have been natural, by its nearest Christian neighbors, the Frankish Church, but by heralds from more distant lands. Severinus Fridold, or Fridolin, and others did much to relay the ruined foundations of religion among the Germanic tribes, but three names stand out most conspicuously, Columbanus, Willibrord, and Winfrid or Boniface. These were all from the British Church, and their zeal and devotion bear witness to the high state of culture and piety in these islands.

Columbanus was born in Ireland in 559, and even as a youth was noted for his scholarship, having performed, among other literary labors, the remarkable task of translating the Book of Psalms from the original Hebrew, in order that what he considered as errors of the Alexandrian or Septuagint translators might be corrected. His missionary zeal, however, was early awakened, and in his thirtieth year with twelve companions he set sail from Ireland, intending to go to Southern Germany. Diverted into France, in the region of Burgundy, he finally found his way to the German frontier and established his headquarters at Anegray and Luxeuil, in the Vosges Mountains. Here he built up strong monastic communities of the type common to those days and from which as a center his missionaries went far and wide among the savage tribes along the head waters of the Rhine and the Rhone. They also went south to the pagan Suevi, the ancestors of the modern Swiss, and with Columbanus' companion and successor, Galbus, did much to firmly re-establish the Church among the hardy mountaineers. At Bregenz on Lake Zurich, idols were destroyed and monasteries founded and the arts of religion and peace were established. Columbanus also attempted to establish himself in Italy, but soon died at the monastery of Bobbio, which he had founded in 615. He was a faithful and fearless champion of the truth, and his stern rebuke of the evil life of Brunhilde, the queen-mother of Burgundy, while it did not, as in the case of John the Baptist, cause him to lose his life, did drive him far from the civilization and comforts of his day, to a life of privation and toil, but also to a work which had great influence upon the spread of Christ's Kingdom.

Willibrord was the missionary apostle of Holland. He was an Englishman by birth, but part of his education and much of his zeal were derived from the Irish Church, under whose influence he came while still young. He sailed for Friesland and landed at the mouth of the Rhine in 690. The land was rough, the people wild, the work difficult, but regardless of obstacles, he labored on year after year, re-enforcing his little band of helpers by new recruits from home until he had firmly laid the foundations of Christianity among a people that were destined in after centuries to be perhaps the most devoted and bold defenders of the Christian faith that have yet been known in the history of the Church, for to Holland of the sixteenth century the whole world owes a spiritual and civic debt that can not soon or easily be repaid.

But of all these Anglo-Saxon missionaries, Winfrid or Boniface was the most distinguished (755). His first journey to other lands was to Frisia, where Willibrord was now growing old and anxious to transfer some of his important work to younger and more vigorous hands. He was offered the bishopric of Utrecht, but turned from these honors and took up instead the difficult and dangerous work of reorganizing the religious and Church life of the widely scattered and independent German tribes. [4]"Five hundred years before, the religion of the cross had followed the Roman eagles along the Roman roads to the Roman camps and towns. The rough and ready Frankish rulers, still half pagan in their ideals, had given it a cast of their own; swarms of zealous Irish missionaries had woven their ideas widely through the fabric," and the resultant was a form of faith which was not pleasing to Rome or wholly in accord with the theological or ecclesiastical needs of the days. "Boniface proved the man for the hour. He converted, organized,

[4] "Two Thousand Years Before Carey," p. 303.

and reorganized the German Churches into the one Church of Rome. The heathen Allemani, Hessians, Bavarians, Saxons, and Franks of the various tribes heard the gospel from him and turned to Christ in great numbers." [5]"It is said that in the course of about twenty years he baptized about 100,000 of the pagan inhabitants of Germany. Although this number is probably much exaggerated and although such wholesale baptisms were not an unmixed good, yet it is evident that it was by his zeal, combined with a singular faculty for organization, that Germany became a professedly Christian land." In his old age he essayed once more to carry the gospel into Holland or Frisia, whence he had withdrawn in his early manhood, and set out with an expedition for that purpose. For a time they succeeded in their work, but soon the savage Frisians determined to rid themselves of their intruders, and there on the shores of the Zuider Zee, at the age of seventy-five, Boniface pillowed his head on a volume of the Gospels and calmly received the sword-stroke that gave him the martyr's crown.

While this work was going on in Central Europe, there were those who penetrated beyond the rivers and forests of France and Germany and Holland to the remoter regions of Denmark and Sweden and even to far-away Greenland. In Denmark and Sweden the pioneer missionary was Anskar (822). He was invited to Denmark by

---

[5] "Medieval Missions," p 114.

King Harold of Jutland, who, in a visit to Louis the Pious, the successor of Charlemagne, had been converted to Christianity. Returning with this king, he established a Christian school, whose advantages, however, were so little appreciated that he had to get his scholars from among slave boys, who were compelled to attend Anskar's instructions. Nevertheless, some progress was made until King Harold, by a revolt of his people, was forced to abdicate his throne, and the work of the missionaries was for the time brought to a close. But while the door was thus shut in Denmark, it was opened in Sweden, "where," as says Neander in his Church History, "some seeds of Christianity had already been scattered. Commerce had especially contributed to this event. Christian merchants had conveyed the knowledge of Christianity to Sweden, and merchants from Sweden, becoming acquainted with Christianity at Dorstede (or Dordrecht, in Holland, which in those days was the great *entrepot* of the Northern trade) had many of them no doubt embraced the faith. Thus the way was opened for Anskar to minister to the Christians already in Denmark and through them to reach their savage and still heathen countrymen. He established his work at Hamburg, on the borders of Germany and Denmark, and in spite of reverses and losses, succeeded in establishing Christianity in both of these northern kingdoms."

Similar work was done in Pomerania by Otto,

who astonished the splendor-loving Russians by the impressiveness of his services and the magnificence of the long line of his richly dressed retinue. It is said of this missionary that "he did little public preaching, but a great many Christlike deeds," which perhaps was not a bad example for his successors in other lands and ages.

"Lief the Lucky" was a son of the Norseman Eric the Red, the reputed discoverer and colonizer of Greenland. Visiting the king of Norway, who was a Christian, Lief was easily led to embrace the faith, and then determined to return to Greenland and Christianize the colonists from Iceland, who had settled there. On his way he was driven to the south by storms and is presumed to have landed on the coast of New England. Thus, though for four hundred years no use was made of this discovery, [6]"the continent of North America was first visited by a Christian Viking bound on an errand from the king of Norway to win the people of Greenland to Christ." On reaching Greenland he established a Christian Church in his father's colony which continued for four hundred years or until the colony was finally abandoned.

During all this time of missionary activity on the part of the Western or Roman Church, the Eastern Church or that portion of Christendom which acknowledged the Patriarch of Con-

[6] "Winners of the World," pp. 5-7.

stantinople as their head, was not moved to any great display of missionary zeal. Perhaps their most noted achievement was in the mission of two Greek priests from Thessalonica, the brothers Cyril and Methodius, by name. Their special work was among the Bulgarians, and the story is that their savage king Bagoris was converted by seeing a picture of the Last Judgment, which Methodius, who was skilled in painting, had depicted upon the wall of the palace. The brother missionaries also did a work more lasting than the conversion of a barbaric king. [7]"'They found the Slavonic race without a written language and constructed for it an alphabet based on the Greek. Having made letters for the Slavs, they gave them a literature. They translated the whole Bible into Slavonian and created a liturgy in that tongue. As Max Müller says, 'This is still the authorized version of the Bible for the Slavonic race and to the student of the Slavonic languages it is what Gothic is to the student of German.' "

But even a greater result of their work was that in thus enabling the Slavs to worship God and to read His Word in their own language, instead of in the Latin, they aroused the antagonism of the more bigoted of the Romish clergy, including the pope, and precipitated the final separation of the Church into its two great divisions of Roman and Greek.

Such are a few examples of the early mis-

---

[7] "Two Thousand Years Before Carey," p. 323.

sionaries and of the character of the work whereby they laid the foundation of the religion which in most of their mission fields has persisted to the present day. It may, however, be useful to gather up the suggestions of these facts into a somewhat general statement and to look at both sides of this work of missions in mediæval and early times, noting very briefly its benefits and its defects.

As to the latter, a recent writer says: [8]"'The aim of these workers throughout this long period (the mediæval) was to bring men under the power of the sacraments and to make them the subject of priestly intercession and manipulation. The missionaries wrought not to make disciples, but to induce men to suffer the clergy to save them through priestly services of magical value.

"The missionary strategy appears in the workers first getting a priestly hold over leaders, kings, nobles, etc., and subsequently prevailing on them to enforce the acceptance of the current Christianity on their subjects: in their attacks on heathen superstitions and gods and, coming off unhurt, arguing the victory of Christ over the god whose honor had been attacked, and in playing generally upon the ignorance and superstition of the people." This writer also instances the decreasing use of the Scriptures in the vernacular and the increasing dependence upon false miracles and the modifying of the gospel to meet the special

8 "Introduction to Christian Missions," pp. 93, 94.

tastes and customs of those to whom they presented it.

Still, although all this and more is probably true, it must be remembered that however imperfect from our twentieth century standpoint these mediæval missions were as to spirit or method, yet they were infinitely superior to any other religious influence then in existence and that their standards of Christian thought and living were a power to raise those who accepted them far above their previous convictions and actions. We are not ourselves as yet so far removed from all crudities and imperfections in the life of so-called Christian peoples, nor even in the methods and work of our missionary endeavors, as to look with entire disapproval upon the work of men, many of whom wrought so faithfully and with such passionate devotion to the light of truth as they saw it. The annals of patristic and mediæval missions, as well as those of the Romish Church of later generations, are full of examples of the most splendid devotion to the cause of Christ as they understood that cause and its requirements in their day.

The methods employed in the Mediæval Age were essentially those of an earlier age, and it is interesting to note that the five methods still largely used by foreign missionary workers were well known to the workers of a thousand years ago—preaching the gospel, medical work, of which the monks were almost the sole practitioners, literary work, whereby the spark of learning was kept alive among the clergy when it had almost died out among the common people, and educational work, for the monasteries and nunneries were the combined common school, high school, and university of the day, without whose efforts a greater ignorance even than that which did prevail would have been inevitable. And finally, the industrial method, so usefully employed to-day, is found at least in its genesis, for, as a writer says:

[9]"A monastery was as a rule an institution competent to supply the temporal necessities of its members. Some of the brothers gave a measure of attention to agriculture and dairying and stock-raising; some to the mechanical arts; some, but in rarer instances, to the fine arts and learning. In the effort to support themselves and their work they became, by example, teachers of the communities around them in many of the arts of civilization and wrought for their material advancement along many lines."

One thing, however, especially marked the missions of this age, in that the "laymen's movement" of the early Church, during which time, as we have seen, every Christian was a missionary, was replaced by a body of missionaries recruited almost wholly from the clergy. Such were Patrick and Columba, founders of the Irish and the Scottish Churches; such were Columbanus and Galbus,

[9] United Editors' Encyclopedia—Article "Monasteries."

who labored in Gaul and Switzerland; such was Augustine of England; such were Willibrord in Holland and Boniface in Germany; such were the apostles to Bulgaria, Cyril and Methodius, and such were the great missionary orders, the Dominicans and Franciscans and Jesuits, whose chief work was the spread of the gospel and the aggrandizement of that Church which to them represented Christianity. Such, too, we may remark in passing, has been until very lately the general trend of even Protestant missions, and we may hail with gratitude and great hopefulness the revival of missionary knowledge and zeal among the laymen of the Protestant Church of to-day, as in a sense a return to those convictions and methods by means of which, for the first three or four centuries of the Christian era, the religion of the Christ swept on to victory.

CHAPTER IV

MEDIÆVAL MISSIONS

In the latter part of the eleventh century arose that remarkable series of events called the Crusades, which might almost be called the "missions militant" of the Christian Church, whose immediate purpose was to rescue the Holy Land and the tomb of Christ from the domination of the Moslems, and whose effects upon the religious, intellectual, and social life of Europe, and ultimately of the civilized world, were both powerful and widespread.

There are usually reckoned in history seven crusades, extending over a period of about one hundred and seventy-five years (1095-1270). Their immediate cause was the oppressions and cruelties wrought by the more fanatical Moslems on Christian pilgrims to the Holy Land, as well as on Christian natives of Syria and surrounding lands. Pope Urban II preached a crusade to avenge the wrongs of these Christians and to rescue the tomb of Christ from the possession of the Moslems, and his exhortations aroused widespread enthusiasm. Thousands from all parts of Christendom enlisted for the Holy War. The war-cry of the advancing hosts was "*Deus Vult*" (God

Wills It), and their armor, shields, and banners were emblazoned with the sign of the cross. The first expeditions consisted of undisciplined and useless material and were wholly unfitted to meet the difficulties they encountered. They never even reached Palestine. Each was overcome by the hardships of the journey or was attacked and cut to pieces by the Mohammedans.

At last (1096) there set forth on their tremendous task six armies of disciplined and well-armed warriors, comprising over 600,000 men, the chivalry and military power of feudal Europe, led by chiefs of experience and renown. They rendezvoused at Constantinople, captured Nice in 1097, Antioch in 1098, and after incredible hardships and sufferings from disease and battle, achieved the great object of the expedition by the capture of Jerusalem in 1099. Godfrey of Bouillon was elected king of Jerusalem and a Christian kingdom erected which finally included all of Palestine, and which withstood the attacks of the surrounding Mohammedan nations for more than fifty years, until it fell before their persistent onslaughts. Repeated attempts were made by the Moslems to recapture Syria and Palestine, and by the Christians to defend these possessions or to take once again those portions that fell before the valor of the Saracenic or Arabian hosts. These succeeding Crusades occurred in 1144, 1189, 1203, 1228, 1244, and 1270. The most holy priests of the Church preached these Crusades, and the mightiest monarchs of Europe and their peoples engaged in them, but little by little the religious fervor grew cool, the political and military rewards of such expeditions became less tempting, and in 1270, with the return from Syria of Prince Edward, afterward Edward I, "the last of the crusaders," the Holy Land and its adjacent territory was gradually repossessed by the Saracens and other Moslem peoples, under whose control it has ever since remained.

As to the effect of the Crusades, while they were in no true sense a missionary movement, yet they spread the knowledge of Christianity among regions in which it had long been unknown, exerted a strong influence upon the life of mediæval and even of modern Europe, and did much in bringing together the East and the West in a way never before possible. As a writer on this subject well says, [1]"While we can not help deploring the enormous expenditure of human life which the Crusades occasioned, it is impossible to overlook the fact that they exercised a most beneficial influence on modern society." Guizot, in his lectures on European civilization, endeavors to show the design and place of the Crusades in the destinies of Christendom. "To the first chroniclers," he says, "and consequently to the first Crusaders of whom they are but the expression, Mohammedans are objects only of hatred; it is evident that those who speak of them do not know

[1] United Editors' Encyclopedia, Article "Crusades."

them. The historians of the later Crusades speak quite differently: it is clear that they look upon them no longer as monsters; that they have to a certain extent entered into their ideas; that they have lived with them; and that relations and even a sort of sympathy have been established between them." Thus the minds of both parties, particularly of the Crusaders, were partly delivered from those prejudices which are the offspring of ignorance. "A step was taken toward the enfranchisement of the human mind." *Secondly,* the Crusaders were brought into contact with two civilizations richer and more advanced than their own, the Greek and the Saracenic; and it is beyond all question that they were much impressed by the wealth and comparative refinement of the East. *Thirdly,* the close relationship between the chief laymen of the West and the Church, inspired by the Crusades, enabled the former to "inspect more narrowly the policy and motives of the papal court." The result was very disastrous to that spirit of veneration and belief on which the Church lived, and in many cases an extraordinary freedom of judgment and hardihood of opinion were induced, such as Europe had never before dreamed of. *Fourthly,* great social changes were brought about. A commerce between the East and the West sprang up, and towns, the early homes of liberty in Europe, began to grow great and powerful. The Crusades indeed "gave maritime commerce the strongest impulse it had ever received." The united effect of these things again, in predisposing the minds of men to a reformation in religion, has been often noticed. Other causes undoubtedly co-operated and in a more direct and decisive manner, but the influence of the Crusades in procuring an audience for Luther can not be overlooked by the philosophic historian.

Although the Crusades did very little directly for the evangelization of the Mohammedans there were those in that age and in the immediately subsequent centuries who ardently desired and endeavored to carry the Christian faith to Moslem peoples. Among those who stand out prominently in these efforts were [2] John of Damascus (760) and Peter the Venerable (1115) who first studied this problem with an intelligent sympathy and advocated the employment of spiritual weapons only against the Moslem, and who prepared for this purpose translations of the Scriptures and other religious works; Raymond Lull (1275), the first to urge the supreme need of special training for the evangelization of Moslems, and who exemplified his contention by his own life of toil and martyrdom; and Francis Xavier (1596) who lived at Lahore, India, while writing a book by which he purpose to prove to Moslems the superiority of Christianity to Mohammedanism.

During the mediæval period, moreover, several monastic orders were formed or specially flourished whose principal purpose was to defend and extend the Christian faith and which may, there-

[2] See Chapter X on Mohammedan Lands.

fore, be rightly called the missionary orders or missionary societies of the Romish Church. Among the best known of these were: The Benedictines, the Franciscans, the Dominicans, and, most famous of all, the Society of Jesus or the Jesuits.

The earliest of these orders was the Benedictines, founded by the father of monasticism in the Western Church, Saint Benedict of Nursia. Its first monastery was established in 529 at Monte Cassino near Naples, and after the sixth century the order increased so rapidly that the Benedictines must be regarded as the main agents in the spread of Christian civilization and learning in the West. They are said to have had at one time as many as 37,000 monasteries, and counted among their branches the great order of Cluny, and the still greater order of the Cistercians, and later still the more modern order of the Trappists. These were popularly known as "the Black Monks," because of the long black gown and cowl that formed the dress of their order. They were particularly flourishing in France, although they had also many monasteries and much wealth in Germany, Spain, Italy, and England. They were chiefly noted as promoters of literature and education, and many eminent writers and translators are numbered in this brotherhood. To them is largely due the preservation of literature during the Dark Ages, and though their direct connection with missionary work was but small, yet by providing a literature which was of value to the spread of Christian civilization, they rendered a service of incalculable value to the development of the religious and literary life of the Middle Ages.

The Franciscans, or Minorites, popularly called the "Gray Friars," in distinction from the "Black Monks" or Benedictines, was an order founded by Saint Francis of Assisi, who is to be carefully distinguished from Saint Francis Xavier. Francis of Assisi was the son of an Italian merchant, who led at first a life of pleasure and worldliness, which he later renounced for the poverty and self-denial of a religious life. In 1208, with seven other companions, he formed a monastic community whose three chief rules were the vows of chastity, poverty, and obedience. The literal interpretation of the vow of poverty would have prohibited the ownership of any property by the order, and over this point many and serious contentions arose which gave rise to other affiliated but less vigorously conducted branches of the order. A very important feature of the order of Franciscans was the enrollment of members who were not bound to live in the monasteries, but who continued to mingle with society without the rule of celibacy or the more stringent regulations of the order. These were called "Tertiaries" or members of the Third Order of St. Francis. They were bound to devote themselves to the works of Christian charity, to serve the sick, to instruct the ignorant, and in a word to practice as far as possible, while living in the world, the virtues of the cloister. In this branch of the order were members of every rank from the throne to the cottage, and their influence counted largely on the religious and social life of their times. In time they also divided into several sub-orders of Franciscans, among which the Recollets are noted as furnishing many of the missionaries sent by the Romish Church to the possessions of France and Spain in the New World after the discovery and early settlement of America.

The Franciscans have always been charged with the defense of the faith of the Romish Church, and one of their greatest theologians was Duns Scotus, whose system of theology still has its influence. Roger Bacon, Cardinal Ximines, and several of the popes of the fourteenth and fifteenth centuries belonged to this order. It is still extant and flourishing and from its ranks have been and are still drawn more of the missionary workers of the Romish Church than from any other monastic order save that of the Jesuits. The beautiful Museè de Cluny in Paris is a former monastery of this order.

The order of the Dominicans or Preaching Friars was founded by Dominic de Guzman, a Spanish priest, to whom was given the task of trying to convert the heretical Albigenses. In the early prosecution of this work he became convinced that a special order, whose duty should be preaching and the cure of souls, was needed in the Romish Church, and in 1216 the order which he founded was confirmed by Pope Honorius III. Failing, however, to convert the Albigenses by peaceable methods, a religious crusade was declared against them and grew into a terrible and bloody war, which lasted for twenty years and in which thousands of persons miserably perished who were innocent of any crime but the belief in that which to the Romish Church was a false faith.

The Dominican order spread very rapidly and they soon became the expounders of the Romish doctrines. The greatest theologian of the Middle Ages, Thomas Aquinas, was a member of this order. They were the chief agents in the Papal Inquisition and strove to convert men by torture where argument had not sufficient effect. As preachers and teachers the order really did much for the propagation of the Romish type of Christianity and spread not only throughout papal countries, but into foreign lands, so that "their monasteries arose throughout Christendom, and even on the shores of Asia, Africa, and subsequently, America."

But the greatest and the most recently formed of all the missionary orders of the Romish Church was and is the order of the Society of Jesus, commonly known as the Jesuits. This order was founded in 1534 by a Spaniard, Ignatius Loyola, and five other associates, the best known of whom was the great missionary Francis Xavier. The first object of this association was a pilgrimage to the Holy Land and a mission to the infidels, but the conditions in Europe arising from the rapid progress of the Reformation modified the first purpose of the founders and led them to add to the usual monastic rules of chastity, poverty, and obedience, a fourth vow by which the members of the order bound themselves to go without question as missionaries to any place to which they might be sent. The rules of this organization, binding them to implicit obedience to the commands of their superiors, are very rigid and their habit of thus "obeying orders" without qualification or questioning has made this order a most powerful instrument for the propagation of the papacy. It is not a conventual order in the same sense as some of the other religious orders of the Church, but through their control of education in the various European countries where they flourished, and especially by their bold penetration of heathen and non-papal lands and the zeal and persistence with which they pushed their teachings and influence, the Jesuits came into practical control not only of the Church, but of the civil government in very many places. This result, together with their invasion of the privileges and influences of the universities and collegiate bodies of Europe, aroused a great opposition to them which culminated in their suppression as an order by Pope Clement XIV (1773). In 1814, however, Pius VII permitted the order to be revived, and they still exist as a powerful influence in the Church, although watched with suspicion and often treated with severity by the several European governments.

We are, however, chiefly concerned with the Jesuits as a missionary order, and in this respect their progress was rapid and influential. In this work [3]"they outstripped all the older orders of the Church. In the Portuguese colonies of India the successes of Francis Xavier are well known. The results of their missions in China were even more extraordinary, as typified by the labors and successes of Matteo Ricci and Johann von Scholl, as they also were in Japan and in North and Central America. Their establishments in South America, as in Brazil, in Paraguay, and Uruguay, on the Pacific Coast in California, and in the Philippines, were missions of civilization as much as of religion." It is, however, to be remembered that so much of the religious teachings of the Jesuits was concerned with the formal observances of religion that many of the peoples "evangelized" by them have sunk back into practical heathenism.

In the United States and Canada the Jesuit missions seem to have been of an higher order than in many other places. Beginning at Quebec in 1625, their missionaries exhibited great bravery and devotion, penetrating the wilderness, preaching to and teaching the most fierce and blood-

[3] **United Editors' Encyclopedia, "Jesuits."**

thirsty Indian tribes, and often falling victims to the passions of savages. The names of Jogues, Breboeuf, Marquette, LaSalle, and others stand out as those of hardy explorers and pioneers and devoted Christian missionaries who without a murmur gave their strength and life for their Indian converts, and the annals of the Jesuit missionaries in Canada and the United States are, as a whole, a bright chapter in the history of this order.

The Roman Catholic Cathedral of St. James at Montreal, Canada, contains an unusual and beautiful memorial of the missionary work of the Romish orders in the magnificent paintings wherein are depicted scenes, not from the lives of the "saints," but from the lives of those who braved the terrors of wilderness and river that as missionaries of Christ they might carry the message of His cross to the savage Indians of those Northern lands. Such a recognition of their bravery and zeal is as well merited as it is unique.

CHAPTER V

MISSIONS IN THE REFORMATION PERIOD

THE beginning of the Reformation of the sixteenth century is customarily dated from 1517. As a fact this was but the culmination of a long series of efforts on the part of men to assert their spiritual and intellectual independence. With the increase of power in the Church and its gradual identification with the civil power abuses had grown up that caused men to pause and wonder, then to think for themselves, and finally to doubt the reliability of the Romish Church or the spirituality of its life and purpose. Cardinal Pole (1500) had said that "men ought to content themselves with their own inward convictions, and not to concern themselves to know if errors and abuses existed in the Church," but with awakening and spreading intelligence and knowledge, this was impossible. There were many "Reformers before the Reformation," such as Wyclif in England (1324), Huss and Jerome of Prague in Bohemia (1369), Reuchlin in Germany (1455), Erasmus in Holland (1465), and many others who protested against the abuses of the Church by argument or ridicule. Finally "the little monk that shook the world," Martin Luther, arose and in his ninety-five theses nailed on the church door at

Wittenberg (1517)[1], challenged the attention of all Europe and set a light to the fire already prepared. Others followed him. Zwingli in Switzerland (1519), Calvin in France (1530), and Knox in Scotland (1560), with scores of less noted leaders, opposed the errors and inconsistencies of Rome and protested against her false teachings and her pernicious power. Not only contests of thought and word, but conflicts of armed men broke out everywhere and all Europe was soon involved in the flames of civil and religious war.

When, after nearly three-quarters of a century, the results of this fierce agitation could be ascertained, the Western Church was found to have been divided into three main bodies, the Romish, the Lutheran, and the Reformed or Calvinistic, of which the latter two have ever since borne the distinctive and common title of Protestant.

The great changes thus accomplished were in the main twofold, doctrinal and governmental. In doctrine these three fundamental facts were asserted and declared to be the foundation of the true Christian faith, viz.:

1. The absolute supremacy of the Scriptures, as opposed to the Romish doctrine of the coordinate authority of tradition and the Councils of the Church.

2. Salvation by faith in Christ alone, as differing from dependence on the ceremonies and absolutions of the Church.

---

[1] October 31, 1517.

3. The essential priesthood of all believers, who therefore require no intermediary between God and man, save Jesus Christ.

The second fruit of the Reformation, the denial of the authority of the Church in civil matters and even of the religious supremacy of the Papacy, manifested itself in the adoption of many varying forms of civic and of Church government and consequent relaxing of ecclesiastical control.

All this was the result of years of argument and contention, of toil and bloodshed, of cruel persecution and of the patient suffering of many, but in the end it wrought out many blessings for the whole world that could not have been otherwise obtained.

One of the results of the Reformation, however, which is somewhat difficult of explanation, was the attitude of the Protestant Church of the Reformation to missions during the Reformation period (1517-1650).

Having been themselves emancipated from the superstitions and slavery of a false doctrine and a harsh ecclesiastical government, it would be thought most natural that the reformers and those who followed them should promptly turn their attention to spreading these glad tidings among non-Christian peoples, but here a strange anomaly is found in the fact that there has been hardly any period in the entire history of the Christian Church so destitute of any concerted effort to spread the gospel in heathen lands than just this period of the Reformation.

Reasons for this strange fact have been given as follows:[1]

1. Immediate intercourse with the heathen nations was not had by the Protestants during this period save, toward its close, in the case of the Dutch and English.

2. The battle against heathenism within old Christendom, the struggle for their own existence against papal and worldly power and the necessity of consolidation at home summoned them primarily to a work which claimed all the energy of young Protestantism.

3. The leading reformers not only did not attempt missionary movements, but they absolutely failed to apprehend the abiding missionary obligation of the Church as set forth in the Scriptures.

Luther held that the obligation to universal missions rested on the apostles alone; that such work had been done long before his age, and that the end of the world was at hand, so that no time remained for the further development and extension of the Kingdom of God on earth.

Melanchthon expressed some of the same views in a more dogmatic form.

Martin Bucer held that the evangelization of the world had not been completed and that God would send "apostles" to the heathen nations, but did not teach that it was the duty of the Church to take up this work.

---

[1] "Introduction to Christian Missions," pp. 130, 131.

Calvin did not deny that much of the world was still to be evangelized, but he laid the obligation of extending the gospel into non-Christian lands not upon the Church, but upon "the Christian magistracy" or the civil government.

In accordance with this latter view, which seems to have been favored by John Knox, some Protestant governments, notably that of Geneva and later of Holland, attempted the founding of Christian colonies in heathen lands. One under Villegagnon went from France to Brazil, but soon failed to accomplish any good. The Dutch Government, in its charter of the Dutch East India Company (1602), stipulated that it should care for the planting of the Church and the conversion of the heathen in its newly acquired territories in Ceylon, Formosa, and Malaysia, but its "conversion" of the heathen was formal and governmental and produced but little permanent results. The Dutch colonies in America had far better success in their religious work with the Indians, many of whom in the vicinity of the Dutch settlements in New York and Albany and elsewhere became earnest and consistent Church members. The "Pilgrim Fathers" also "adopted the conversion of the native heathen into their colonial program," and the fruitful labors of Eliot and Brainerd and the Mayhews are notable in missionary annals.

But if the early Reformation Church as a body did but little missionary work, there were those who did not fail to see the light and proclaim the truth in this matter. Among the earliest to arouse the Church to a sense of her real duty toward the unevangelized world was a layman, the Baron Justinian Von Welz (1664), who by a series of pamphlets argued that the Church had no right to confine her ministrations to nominal Christians, but was in duty bound to send the gospel to all who had either not yet heard it, or hearing had not heeded its voice. He wrote three separate treatises in support of his position and argued his views before the Imperial Diet at Ratisbon, but after years of effort, failing to move the Church, he personally received consecration and went as a missionary to Dutch Guiana, there to fill a lonely grave. His pleas and arguments seemed to have been fruitless, but as the corn of wheat which, dying, brings forth fruit, so his views were of much value to the missionary cause in after years.

Another movement which followed that of the great spiritual rebellion against the errors of Rome, and took place within the Protestant Church itself in both its branches, gave a new spirit and power to the cause of missions. [2]"It was in the age of Pietism that missions struck their first deep roots and it is the spirit of Pietism which, after Rationalism had laid its hoar frost on the first blossoming, again revived them and has brought them to their present bloom." [3]Francke, the great Pietist of his generation, did more than any other man of that time to beget the missionary spirit, seek out missionaries and find congrega-

---

[2] "History of Protestant Missions"—Warneck.

[3] "Introduction to Christian Missions," p. 145.

tions in the fatherland which, by their contributions, would support them. Barnes calls him "the forefather of modern missions." One of the earliest of modern missionary training schools was established under his influence at Halle, and through his advice, if not by his direct appointment, such leaders of missions as Ziegenbalg and Plutschau went forth from the Danish Church to lay in India the foundations of modern missions.

Count Zinzendorf, the reviver and great leader of the Moravian Brethren, was also educated in Francke's institution at Halle, and was thus influenced even as a boy to regard with interest the great work of carrying the gospel to the heathen. Later he became the leader among those wonderfully consecrated people, the United Brethren, or Moravians, whose missionary work is the marvel of the world even down to our day.

In the ranks of the Danish Halle missions, besides those mentioned, we find such names as that of Christian Frederick Schwartz in India (1750), who was so unaffectedly devoted to the welfare of his converts that "on the occasion of a formidable native rising under the haughty Mohammedan Hyder Ali, that potentate refused to treat with an English embassy, but said, 'Send me the Christian (Schwartz); he will not deceive me.'" At his death a magnificent memorial marble, by the English sculptor Flaxman, was erected over his grave by the Rajah of Tanjore, who from his youth had been his pupil and his confiding friend.

Nor must we forget to mention Hans Egede, the intrepid Danish missionary to the Eskimos of Greenland, whose privations and zeal made him the founder of Christian missions in that desolate land, although, as is often the case, the real success of his work did not become apparent until after he himself had passed away (1758).

Crossing the Atlantic, we find that the missionary work of Roger Williams (1631), the founder of Rhode Island, is worthy of special note. While he was assistant pastor at Plymouth, he devoted himself largely to the Indians, living in their lodges and learning their language so as to use it freely. He published an Indian-English vocabulary and phrase-book of the language in use among some of the New England tribes. His ultimate purpose was the conversion of the Indians, and his defense of some of their rights as against the aggressions of the colonists gave him great influence among them.

But perhaps the best known names of early missionaries to the North American Indians are those of John Eliot, David Brainerd, and the Mayhew family.

[4]"Eliot began his work in 1646, preaching to a band of Indians at Nonatuc, near Roxbury, Massachusetts. It was largely because of the interest excited in England by Eliot's work that a missionary society was organized in England, 'The Society for the Propagation of the Gospel

---

[4]"Two Thousand Years Before Carey," p. 409.

in New England' (1649). This first English society was organized one hundred and forty-eight years before the society inspired by William Carey, and did much to encourage and support the work of Carey and his fellows. Its work, with a largely increased scope, was later taken over by the Society for the Propagation of the Gospel in Foreign Parts (1701)."

Eliot's monumental work was the translation of the Bible into Indian (1661-63). He trained his converts by gathering them into Christian villages, and in 1670 he had thus instituted nine "Praying Towns," the first one of which was organized at Natick, near Boston. [5]"'Here the Christian Indian could go to a church where an Indian pastor preached, and to a school where an Indian teacher taught, and could live a Christian life free from the persecutions of the heathen Indians about them. The Indians who came to this town made a covenant as follows: 'The grace of Christ helping us, we do give ourselves and our children to God to be His people. He shall rule over us in all our affairs, not only in our religion and affairs of the Church, but also in all our works and affairs of this world.'" In 1674 Eliot had over 1,100 Christian Indians under his immediate care. He lived to see twenty-four of his Christian Indians become preachers of the gospel. His translation of the New Testament was printed in 1661, and that of the Old Testament followed in

---

[5] "Winners of the World," p 90.

1663. His original works were an Indian Catechism, an Indian Psalter, a Primer, and the Indian Grammar. It was at the end of this latter work that he wrote his famous motto, "Prayer and pains, through faith in Jesus Christ, will do anything." He died in 1690, at the venerable age of eighty-six years.

David Brainerd was a man of a singularly beautiful and spiritual character, who finished his life work within a very few years. He began his work among the Indians on the Hudson River, sixteen miles from Stockbridge, Mass. (1743), but his chief work was done among the tribes of northern New Jersey and on the Delaware River, to reach whom he made many long and hazardous journeys. He soon broke down under the hardships of his self-denying life and died at the early age of twenty-nine years, after an active missionary career of only four years. He had been engaged to be married to one of the daughters of the famous preacher and theologian Jonathan Edwards, and it was at his home in Northampton, Mass., that this earnest young Christian finished his course. It has been well said of Brainerd that [6]"he was not remarkable for his learning, he accomplished no great and widespread results in the field which he had chosen, but the journal of his daily life and spiritual experiences, which he kept with care and which was published in 1746 by the Scottish Society that supported him, is full of life and power to this day. In reading it the

[6] Encyclopedia of Missions, "David Brainerd."

man's character, his lofty principles and aims, his saintliness, his loyalty to Jesus Christ, and his perseverance under hardships do not fail to impress the reader and to arouse the desire to follow his example. It was this fine and zealous character of Brainerd which made Jonathan Edwards a missionary to the Indians of Stockbridge; it was to Brainerd's memoirs to which Henry Martyn traced his decision to become a missionary, and it was also to those simple records of a godly life that William Carey was indebted for much of that inspiration which shaped his decision to be a missionary. Brainerd was a truly noble man and a Christian hero of that small class of heroes whose lives seem to shape history."

The missionary record of the [7]Mayhew family holds a unique place in the annals of Christian missions. Thomas Mayhew, Sr., had been a merchant in Southampton, England. In 1641 he obtained a grant of the islands now called Martha's Vineyard, Nantucket and the neighboring Elizabeth Islands, off the southern coast of Massachusetts, and became a proprietor of these islands and governor of the colonists who settled there. His son, Thomas Mayhew, Jr., was pastor of the colonists' church and soon took up missionary work for the native tribes that occupied the island. Within ten years an Indian church of 282 members was organized. He went to England to solicit funds for this work and was lost at sea. His aged father, then over seventy years of age,

---

[7] "Two Thousand Years Before Carey," pp. 410, 411.

took up the work, learned the language of the Indians, and devoted himself to their welfare, "often walking twenty miles through the woods to preach to or visit these Indians." John Mayhew, the son of Thomas Mayhew, Jr., assisted his grandfather and succeeded to his and his own father's work. His son, Experience Mayhew, was in the work for upward of thirty years and prepared for his Indian flock a new version of the Psalms and of the Gospel of John, besides writing a "Brief Account of the State of the Indians on Martha's Vineyard," etc. His son, Zechariah, was ordained as pastor to these tribes in 1767, and continued his work among them till his death in 1806, thus carrying this remarkable record to the unusual period of one hundred and sixty consecutive years of missionary work by members of the same family to the same people. This instance is said to be paralleled only by that of the family of the Moravian missionary, Frederick Bönisch, which, during five generations, continued similar work for one hundred and forty consecutive years.

These, of course, were but a few of those who, from their sense of obligation to the spiritual welfare of their fellow-men, were pioneers in the modern missionary movement, which has been so blessed and prospered of God. Their work, as we have seen, brings us down to the period of "Modern Missions," which is usually reckoned to have commenced with the remarkable career of William Carey (1793).

With his life and work the hitherto comparatively narrow stream of missionary work begins to widen and deepen and to pour its reviving waters through the world till it has now reached almost every known and habitable land upon the face of the globe. To trace this stream through all its windings or in the details of its course in various lands will not be attempted. The most that can be done is to indicate the development of the great movements and to mention some of the chief leaders of Christian thought in the main mission fields of the modern world. Many fields of great interest and importance can not even be named and many workers of eminent worth must be passed over in silence.

CHAPTER VI

INDIA

THE first Christian missionaries to India came from Egypt. Tradition affirms that the Apostle Thomas went to India and there suffered martyrdom, but the earliest recorded missionary was Pantaenus of Alexandria, who founded a Christian community on the Malabar Coast, while Syrian Christians from the Nestorian Church established a mission on the Eastern or Coromandel Coast of South India during the third century.

Roman Catholic missions did not begin until about 1500, and had to contend not only with the pagan customs and beliefs, but with the fierce hostility of Mohammedanism, which had obtained a firm hold upon the country. Francis Xavier, the Jesuit, landed in Goa, the center of Portuguese India, in 1543, and the Church soon obtained a foothold among the natives that has grown into a quite widespread and powerful Catholic community, which is said to be larger than that of the Protestant Christians and to number about 1,200,000 members.

The Protestant missionary history of India in the period of modern missions begins with the life and work of William Carey. This remarkable man, justly named "the father of modern missions," was born in Paulerspury, Northamptonshire, England, in 1761. He was the son of a poor weaver, but learned the shoemaking trade, at which he worked for twelve years. At the age of eighteen he was converted, joined the Baptist Church, and later became a preacher in that connection, being pastor of the congregation at Moulton. As his support was too meager for the necessities of his family, he continued to make and "cobble" or repair shoes to eke out a livelihood. He was almost wholly self-educated, but became remarkably well learned, acquiring a good knowledge of Latin, Greek, Hebrew, Dutch, and French, besides a large amount of general information. He was early impressed with the duty of the Church to carry the gospel to the unconverted in other lands and frequently urged this subject, but met with scant sympathy among his fellow Christians. At last, at a meeting of the (Baptist) Ministers' Association at Nottingham, England, May 31, 1792, he preached a remarkable sermon from Isa. 54:2, 3, which served as a trumpet call to some who had been heedless of their missionary obligations. His well-known divisions of the sermon were, "Expect great things from God" and "Attempt great things for God." At the conclusion of the discourse twelve of the ministers who heard it withdrew and formed the first Baptist Missionary Society. Its first capital, subscribed by these men, was £13 2s 6d or about $65.72. From such a feeble beginning how great things have come!

Carey offered himself as the first missionary of this society and desired to go to the Sandwich Islands or to West Africa, but on the representations of Dr. John Thomas, a surgeon, who had been engaged in missionary work in Bengal, it was decided to send Carey to India. He was refused passage in an English vessel because the East India Company would not countenance "any interference with the religion of the natives," but sailed in a Danish vessel from Copenhagen to Serampore and finally reached Calcutta, November 11, 1793. From this date is frequently reckoned the beginning of the period of "Modern Missions."

Carey believed in the principle of self-support for missionaries, which, however, has since proven only partially successful in actual experience, and so, relinquishing his salary from the society, he took the post of superintendent of an indigo factory at Malda. This position enabled him to support himself and yet devote much of his time to missionary labors. During the five years he remained here he translated the New Testament into Bengali, held daily religious services for the thousand workmen in the factory, and itinerated regularly through the district, which was twenty miles square and contained two hundred villages. In 1799, Joshua Marshman and William Ward were sent out by the English Baptist Society, but, as in the case of Carey, found themselves barred from British territory. They went to the Danish settlement of Serampore, and were there joined by Carey, thus forming the famous "Serampore Triad." Later an English institution, "Fort William College," was established at Calcutta, and the governor-general, whose favorable notice had been attracted to Mr. Carey because of his linguistic ability, appointed him professor of Sanscrit, Bengali, and Marathi in that college. He devoted most of the salary of $7,500, which was attached to this position, to his missionary work, and with his co-laborers, Messrs. Marshman and Ward, lived on a very modest allowance.[1] These three men may be justly regarded as missionary statesmen and apostles. They laid the foundation for almost every method of subsequent missionary activity by founding schools and colleges, by organizing native preachers and lay workers, and by exercising the right of petition against the crimes committed in the name of the Hindu religion. Carey, whose success as a translator has won for him the title of "the Wycliff of the East," completed a Bengali dictionary in three volumes, and translated the Bible or some of its parts into thirty-six dialects. He prepared grammars and dictionaries in the Sanscrit, Marathi, Bengali, Punjabi, and Telugu dialects. His fame as a botanist was second only to his reputation as a linguist.

---

[1] "Lux Christi," pp. 48, 49.

[2] "'He will also long be remembered as the man through whose influence many idolatrous customs were abolished. In 1801 he secured the passage of a law which prevented mothers from sacrificing their children by throwing them into the Ganges River, and for years he labored to secure from the British Government the abolition of the inhuman 'suttee,' or the practice of burning widows on the funeral pyres of their husbands. At last (1829) the Government sent to him for translation the proclamation putting a stop to this practice. It arrived on a Sunday, as he was about to preach in the church at his station. He immediately sent another man into the pulpit, saying, 'The delay of an hour may mean the sacrifice of many a widow,' threw off his coat, and by sunset had finished the translation of the edict.'' His long residence of forty-one years in India proved him a man of extraordinary intellectual power, accompanied by the rarest humility and most unfaltering devotion to his Master Jesus Christ, and with a consuming love for his fellowmen. It may be fairly said that the conceptions of Carey and of his associates as to the duty and methods of the introduction of Christianity among a non-Christian people have for a century dominated Protestant missions. He died June 9, 1834, at the age of seventy-three.

Eleven years after Carey sailed for India, one of his great successors, Alexander Duff, was born

---

[2] "Winners of the World," p. 73.

(1806) in Perthshire, Scotland. Graduating from the University of St. Andrews at Glasgow, and coming under the influence of Dr. Chalmers, Duff was appointed the first missionary of the newly organized Society of the Church of Scotland, and embarked for India in 1829, at the age of twenty-three. He was thrice wrecked on his voyage, but finally reached Calcutta in safety after a voyage of eight months. He went out as an educational missionary, and the first school which he began "was organized on two great principles: 1. That the Christian Scriptures should be read in every class and be the foundation and pervading salt of the entire school. 2. That since the vernaculars of India could not supply the medium for all the requisite instruction, the sciences of the West should be taught through the English language." These principles were opposed by the scholars and educators then at work in India, and even by the friends of Christian education, but were insisted on by Mr. Duff, who began such a school in 1830, in a building also occupied by the school of a high caste Brahman, Rammohun Roy, who had broken away from the corruptions of Brahmanism and was then at the head of a Reform party. [3]"On the morning when Mr. Duff opened his school, expecting opposition to his plan for Bible readings, he had fortified himself by procuring copies of the Gospel in Bengali and also by learning the Lord's Prayer in Bengali. The moment came.

[3] "Pioneer Missionaries of the Church," p. 105.

Unflinchingly he stood before them and phrase after phrase of that prayer was unfalteringly uttered and dutifully repeated by the pupils. His personal magnetism together with his strength and firmness carried them all, word by word, to its close. Then came the most critical test. With no sign of weakness or distrust, he distributed copies of the Gospels and requested a pupil to read. Silence followed. An unmistakable disgust was discernible on the faces of the superstitious pupils. A threatening murmur of rebellion arose against the contaminating books, when instantly Rammohun Roy arose and in the kindest of tones said to the pupils: 'I have read this entire Bible all through. I received no harm from it. You will receive no harm from it.' Words of assurance followed, and when he finished speaking the students were ready to read the Gospels. A victory was won, and from this began Mr. Duff's startling inroads on the prejudices and superstitions of Hindu families."

In less than a week there were three hundred applicants for admission. Within a year this number was tripled, and in nine years the average attendance was 800, and the school and its methods received the commendation of the governor-general, Lord Bentinck. On the essential principles laid down by Dr. Duff,—the prominence of the Bible in the course of instruction and considerable use of the English language, the largest and most successful Christian schools and colleges in India are now conducted.

Dr. Duff returned home several times and traveled through the Churches of Scotland in the interests of Christian education in India. In 1854 he visited the United States, arousing the greatest enthusiasm toward missionary work. In 1846 he was offered the principalship and chair of theology in the Free Church College at Edinburgh, but though urged by influential men and bodies to take up the work, he steadfastly declined to leave India. However, his failing health at last compelling him to cease his work in India, he accepted the Free Church professorship of theology in 1867, and died in 1878, greatly honored and beloved by all who knew of his remarkable work for Christian education in India.

Henry Martyn, born at Truro, Cornwall, England, in 1781, was graduated at Cambridge with the highest honors, and soon after, abandoning his intention of studying for the bar, prepared to enter the ministry. Influenced by the lives of William Carey and David Brainerd, the missionary to the North American Indians, Martyn determined to devote himself to missionary work, but, through force of circumstances, was obliged to accept an appoinment as a chaplain of the East India Company.

His chief work was that of translation, his linguistic powers being very great. His Persian and Arabic New Testaments were the first complete translations of the Christian Scriptures into these languages. His versions of the New Testament in Hindustani and Persian, spoken by many millions of people, are enduring monuments not only to his scholarship, but to his Christian zeal. He was noted for his earnest piety, his endurance of hardships, rendered doubly severe through his frequent illnesses, and a peculiarly sweet and tender nature that betokened itself in all his relations to others. His early death, the result of too great exertions and an unavoidable exposure to the plague while traveling in Persia, was brought about at the early age of thirty-two in 1812. The influence of his saintly character is still felt in the Christian Church, and is voiced by the inscription on his tombstone in letters of English, Armenian, Turkish, and Persian, "One who was known in the East as a 'Man of God.'"

Bishop Reginald Heber, an early missionary of the Church of England to India and second Bishop of Calcutta, [4]"'united the zeal and piety of the Christian with the accomplishments of the scholar and gentleman. Few men have ever won in equal measure the general esteem of society in India." He was elected Bishop of Calcutta in 1823, and began his duties with great zeal and devotion. His work lasted, however, less than three years, as he died from entering a cold bath while overheated. He is chiefly known to us through his wonderful hymns, such as "Holy, Holy, Holy, Lord God Almighty," "The Son of God Goes Forth to War," and especially "From Greenland's Icy Mountains," which is known and sung throughout

---

[4] "Lux Christi," p. 146.

the Protestant Church, and which was composed in 1819 for use at a missionary service held in a parish church in England. "As the most learned and zealous of Indian bishops he is enshrined in the affections of the Christian world."

These four men, types of their several lines of thought and effort, stand out as grand specimens of the early missionaries sent by the English and Scottish Churches to India, but about this time the religious life of America was also stirred by the same zeal for souls, and in the four men whose names follow her special contributions to India missions will be noted.

Adoniram Judson, who as a student in Andover Theological Seminary had met Mills, Richards, and Hall, members of the famous "Haystack Band" of Williams College, resolved to offer himself as a missionary to the heathen, and after a visit to England in a fruitless effort to enlist the co-operation of the London Missionary Society with the recently organized "American Board," he sailed in 1812 as a missionary of the latter Board to India. During his long voyage, however, his views as to the Scriptural authority for infant baptism were changed and, becoming attached to the Baptist Church, he was the cause of the formation of the American Baptist Missionary Union (1814). Judson at first attempted to work in Madras, but was discouraged by the hostile policy of the British East India Company, and soon removed to Rangoon in Burma, and later to Maulmain, which became the center of the Baptist missionary work in Burma. He suffered much persecution during his early life in Burma. Suspected of being an English spy in a war between Burma and England, he was arrested and for seventeen months confined in the loathsome jails of Ava and Oung-pen-la, where he lay bound in fetters and suffering excruciatingly from fever, heat, hunger, and the cruelty of his keepers. By the persistent efforts of his wife, and the intervention of the British military authorities, he was finally released and resumed his work. He not only labored at the usual tasks of missionary workers, but translated the Bible into Burmese, and commenced the preparation of a Burman dictionary, which monumental work he was not able to fully complete before his death in 1850. "Numerous converts, a corps of trained native assistants, the translation of the Bible and other valuable books into Burmese, and his almost completed Burman-English dictionary were some of the direct fruits of his thirty-seven years of missionary service."

Scarcely less famous or useful in the early history of Indian missions were Dr. Judson's three wives, Ann Hasseltine Judson, Sarah Hall (Boardman) Judson, and Emily Chubbuck Judson. The devotion of the first named wife during the persecutions and sufferings of her husband's earlier life was great, and she labored incessantly at much personal risk and under many hardships to secure his release from his Burman prison.

During his imprisonment, though burdened with the care of her own infant and also with the oversight of a native child who was ill with the smallpox, she constantly visited her heroic husband, brought him suitable food, and with her fortitude and courage sustained him until he was set free. The second wife, who was the widow of Dr. George Dana Boardman, a colleague of Dr. Judson, did most valuable work among the Burmese women and was indeed a pioneer in "women's work for women" in India. Emily Judson, who married Dr. Judson during his last visit to America, was a popular writer of no little renown in her day, writing under the pseudonym of "Fannie Forester." She gave much time to the preparation of a memoir of her distinguished husband. She returned to America after Dr. Judson's death and lived for some years in her former home.

In the early history of India missions the value of medical missions was not fully recognized as an adjunct to the spiritual work which it is so well fitted to advance. It was first given to John Scudder, M. D., of the American Board, to labor effectively in the introduction of this powerful auxiliary to Christian missions among the people of India.

Dr. Scudder was a young physician with a large and promising practice in New York City. One day while waiting to see a patient he picked up a tract on missions entitled "The Conversion of the World," written by Newman and Hall of the Haystack Band, by reading which he was led to give his life to missionary work. He was a member of the Reformed Dutch Church, which was then working in co-operation with the American Board. To the latter Society therefore Dr. Scudder offered his services and sailed with his young wife for Ceylon in 1819. He was ordained as a minister by his fellow missionaries in 1821, and did much of the usual evangelistic work which was then the chief method of missionary endeavor.

But that which distinguished Dr. Scudder from all his contemporaries was the fact that he constantly combined the practice of medicine and surgery with preaching and teaching among the natives. He thus became the first distinctively medical missionary to India and possibly to any foreign field. His method of medical work was largely that of itineration, traveling from village to village, gathering the natives together and preaching the gospel and treating their physical ailments, thus almost exactly following the method pursued by the Master Himself, of whom we read, [5]"He went about all Galilee, teaching in their synagogues and preaching the gospel of the Kingdom and healing all manner of sickness and all manner of disease among the people." Early in 1836 he was sent with Dr. Winslow to Madras to found a new mission, which, in 1853, under the labors of Dr. Scudder's oldest son, the Rev. Dr. Henry Martyn Scudder, M. D., with his

[5] Matt. 4:23.

two brothers, William W. and Joseph, was divided into the Madras and Arcot missions. Ezekiel, Jared W., and John Scudder, Jr., all sons of Dr. Scudder, Sr., with Jacob Chamberlain and Joseph Mayou, joined the mission between the years 1856 and 1861, and from that date on the Scudder and Chamberlain families, to the second and third generations, have been the leading workers in this important district. Medical work has always been one of the chief instruments of this mission, no less than six out of the nine men who may be regarded as the founders of the mission having been qualified physicians. The Arcot Mission may thus be said to have been the pioneer and, in a sense, the leading medical mission of South India.

The work of the Baptist Society among the Telugus in the Madras District is one of the many remarkable instances of the long delayed fruit of faithful labors for the evangelization of non-Christian people. The missions in Nellore and Ongole were established in 1836, but for seventeen years remained so unproductive that the society was on the point of abandoning them and only hesitated because of the faith and patience of the pioneer missionaries, Drs. Day and Jewett. The feeling, however, in favor of discontinuing the work was strong, and while at a Conference of the society the question was being once more debated, the reading of a thrilling poem, naming Nellore "The Lone Star Mission," and written by Dr. S. F. Smith, the author of "America," caused a sudden revulsion of feeling and it was resolved to reinforce the mission. Dr. and Mrs. John E. Clough were sent there, and a few years later the reward of faith was made manifest by [6]"one of the most marvelous mass movements in the history of India missions. In a single day one thousand converts brought their idols to the missionaries in Ongole to be destroyed; on another day, 2,222 were baptized, and at one time 8,691 professed their faith in Christ within the space of ten days."

Among these leaders in India missions we must name Dr. William Butler, because he it was who laid the foundations of the large and increasing work now done in India by the American Methodist Episcopal Church. He arrived in India in 1856 and established his first station at Bareli, near Lucknow. Within ten weeks of the commencement of his work the terrible Sepoy mutiny broke out and he and his family were obliged to flee for their lives and for a long time were in hiding at Naini Tal. "On his return to his station in 1858, three missionaries, one European helper, and two natives answered the roll. Yet to this missionary was given the joy of living until he could see one hundred thousand of the people of India accepting Christ as Lord, brought into this new life through the agency of the Methodist missions." To this great work the labors

---

6 "Lux Christi," p. 15.

of Dr. Parker, Bishop William Taylor, Bishop Thoburn, and many more largely contributed. [7]"Bishop Taylor's masterly evangelistic genius and the revival under him in South India made new centers in Bombay, in Poona, in Secunderabad, in Madras, and in Calcutta. The work was then pushed eastward as far as Rangoon, Methodists thus coming to share with Baptists and Anglicans the work of evangelizing Burma; points of vantage were seized in the Punjab and in the Central Provinces—in fine, the Methodists now survey all India as their field."

While "women's work for women" in India, as elsewhere, has accompanied and followed the work inaugurated by the men, there are some features of this work to which special reference should be made. Some of the peculiar features of the social life of India affect most terribly the physical and moral condition of its women. "The hall-mark of modern Hinduism," as one says, "is the degradation of women." [8]"The chief of the social wrongs of the women of India are, in brief, her marriage in infancy to a man chosen arbitrarily for her, her possible child-widowhood, her entering into married life at ten or twelve years of age, the physical injuries of premature motherhood, combined with neglect of all proper treatment, her absolute ignorance, and her enforced and unnatural seclusion. To these must be added the nameless evils of polygamy and concubinage,

[7] "Lux Christi," p. 163. [8] "Lux Christi," p. 185

the possible doom of infanticide, and the low moral tone of the family life." Against these and similar evils the earliest missionaries protested and worked. William Carey, as we have seen, was successful in obtaining Government prohibition of female infanticide, and also an act forbidding the practice of suttee or burning widows upon the funeral pyre of their dead husbands. Much later (in 1891) a bill was passed raising the age of consent to marriage from ten to twelve years of age. Notwithstanding these laws, their beneficent purpose is often frustrated by the inexorable power of superstition and custom.

The earliest direct work for the women of India was done by Mrs. Marshman in Serampore in 1800. Mrs. Sarah Judson labored among the Burmese girls, and others of the wives of the early missionaries labored faithfully to raise and benefit their own sex in heathen lands, as indeed has ever been their practice.

Miss M. A. Cooke was the first single woman to enter India as a missionary, being sent out by the Church Missionary Society in 1820. She was engaged in educational work for girls, which she very successfully carried on for many years, establishing many schools for girls, and later a female orphanage. She became the wife of the Rev. Isaac Wilson, but never ceased her active efforts in her chosen field.

"Zenana work" or the personal visitation of

the high-class Hindu women in their own homes has naturally been the exclusive work of women missionaries, since the customs of India forbid the free intercourse of the sexes as in Europe and America. [9]"'In this close heart-to-heart encounter the Christian missionary learns the needs and sorrows of India's oppressed wives and mothers. Here in the very deepest part of it, absolutely closed to men missionaries, the family life in all its multiform misery can be reached with the healing and purifying touch of Christianity. Empty-headed, frivolous, and lifeless as is the ordinary Hindu or Mohammedan woman, she is yet within reach of the motives which the missionary thus brings to bear upon her and great have been the results in leading such as these to Christ. There are now estimated to be fifty thousand zenanas in India open to the visits of the Christian missionary, but there are yet forty millions of women in zenanas who can be reached by no other agency."

In education women's work is of supreme importance, and as the utmost care is taken that the secular side does not overshadow the religious, the Christian schools are the seed-beds of the native Church. In the primary schools and kindergartens the girls receive equal attention with the little boys, and in the high schools manual training courses are mingled with those purely literary. There are two Christian colleges for

[9] "Lux Christi," p. 203.

women, the oldest being that at Lucknow, under the care of the American Methodists, and the other the Sarah Tucker College, in Palamcotta, South India, under the Church Missionary Society. The Government colleges are also opened to women, and in about thirty years (1870-1899) 1,306 women passed the entrance examination.

As an example of the "finished product" of Indian female education we need mention only Miss Lilavati Singh, of whom the late Ex-President Harrison said, at the World's Missionary Conference in 1900, "If I had given a million dollars to foreign missions, I should count it wisely invested if it led only to the conversion of that one woman." Mrs. Sarabji and her daughters, the well-known educators of Parsi women, and the world-renowned Pundita Ramabai are conspicuous examples of the benefits of Christian education of Indian women.

Miss Clara Swain, M. D., was sent out in 1869 as the first woman medical missionary to India. She formed a class of sixteen girls for the study of medicine, of which thirteen in due time became qualified practitioners. She also secured the erection of an adequate dispensary and hospital for women. The Nawab of Rampore gave land worth $15,000 for this purpose, and the cost of the buildings was met by the Methodist Women's Society at home. Dispensary cards are distributed bearing verses of Scripture, and Bible women work among the patients while they wait their turn with the doctors.

Certain forward movements in later years give promise of a rich fruitage from the labors of the past. The spiritual unity of Christians has been emphasized by the formation of the South India United Church (1908), a union of all Christians of the Presbyterian and Congregational Missions in South India.

A Women's Missionary College has been recently organized in Madras by the co-operation of no less than ten British and American Missionary Societies. A National Missionary Council, with Provincial Representative Councils in each of the great provinces of India, has lately been constituted to consider and co-operate in plans of mutual importance and interest.

The life of India has also been deeply stirred of late by the awakening of its social conscience and its desire for social service. Two or three great issues have particularly held its attention—such as the education and elevation of women, the condition of the depressed classes and evils resulting from the caste system. The need of education is particularly emphasized. In 1912-1913 the total increase of pupils in British India was nearly 400,000, yet only twenty-nine per cent of the boys and five per cent of the girls of school-going age are at school. All these and other similar movements are having a mighty influence upon the religious, social and political life of India.

CHAPTER VII

CHINA

China, the oldest, the largest, and the most populous of Asiatic countries, has been for centuries a missionary problem. Its authentic history dates back to the times contemporaneous with the rise of Greece and Rome, the fall of Troy, and the days of David and Solomon in Israel.

The area of this great land covers one-third of the entire area of Asia, and equals that of the United States, plus the provinces of Ontario and Quebec in Canada and all of Mexico, to a point beyond the Isthmus of Tehuantepec, or, roughly speaking, about 4,225,000 square miles. The area of China proper, however, is only about one-third of the whole empire. This portion is nearly the size of the United States east of the Rocky Mountains.

Parts of this area are among the most thickly populated on the face of the globe, and although an accurate census of the inhabitants of China has never yet been made, it is estimated at from [1]360,000,000 to [2]386,000,000, [3]426,000,000, or even [4]446,000,000. This is almost one-fourth of

[1] "Rex Christus," p. 3. [2] Warneck, p. 334. [3] Editors' Encyclopedia.
[4] Beach, "Geography of Protestant Missions," p. 262.

the total population of the globe. [5]"This vast population has as one of its most striking characteristics its homogeneity. A common written language, and uniform customs and religions, together with their isolation for ages from surrounding nations, have made this people a practical unit. A patriarchal government based intellectually upon a common literature which is the stepping-stone to all official employment, has welded them together with iron bands, so that to-day they present a united front to the powers of the West."

The reliable history of Christian missions in this great country begins with the entrance of the Nestorians, in 505 A. D., to which testimony is borne by the discovery of the famous Nestorian Tablet, which was found in Hsí-Ngan-Fu in 1625, by workmen engaged in digging for the foundations of a house. The date of this tablet is 781 A. D., which is generally accepted as authentic, and Nestorian Christians seem to have labored in China for upwards of 800 years.

Roman Catholic missions commenced with the work of John of Monte Corvino, an Italian monk, who went on a mission to the Tartars, reaching China about 1298. He built a church at Peking in the tower of which were three bells which were rung at all the canonical hours. He also bought one hundred and fifty slave boys, whom he taught Latin and Greek. He taught these boys to copy

---

5 "Geography of Protestant Missions," p. 263.

manuscript, and especially to chant the services of the Church, and he tells us that the emperor of China used often to come and hear them sing and was greatly pleased with their performance. He also did an important work in translating the New Testament and Psalms into Chinese. In 1308 he was reinforced by three Franciscan monks, and they were followed by other faithful men. But on the fall of the Mongol dynasty, which had favored the Christians, the new rulers of the Ming dynasty put a stop to all communication with foreign lands, and the Christians were persecuted and slain, so that for nearly two hundred years Christianity in China was practically dead and forgotten. Then came the great Jesuit missionary St. Francis Xavier, who made desperate but unavailing attempts to obtain a permanent foothold in the empire (1553), and he was followed thirty years later by "one whose brilliant career in China perhaps has never been equaled by any other missionary in any land—Matteo Ricci. With another Jesuit named Ruggereo, he effected an entrance into the province of Kuang-tung, in 1582, by concealing their purpose and adopting the garb of Buddhist priests. After many years of labor these men and their companions achieved much success and influence, particularly as educators and teachers of Western science, literature, etc. But later they became involved in doctrinal difficulties among themselves and in political and other disputes with the

Chinese authorities, which early in the eighteenth century, and even as late as 1747, led to violent persecutions which for a while almost annihilated Christianity in China. In common with other foreign religions, the Catholic missions shared the benefits of the Treaty of Tient-sin (1858), and now report over 1,100,000 members in China.

Protestant missions to China began with the work of Robert Morrison. Like Carey, he was a shoemaker, or rather a shoe-last maker, and studied while at work at this humble trade. He studied Latin, Hebrew, and theology with the minister of his home parish, New Castle, England, and after some years of preparatory work, in which was included the study of Chinese, he sailed for China, via New York (1807), being unable to go directly to China because of the opposition of the East India Company to missionary work in the East. In this respect Morrison's early difficulties resembled those of Carey.

The American ship in which Morrison sailed from New York was owned by Olyphant and Co., a firm of Christian merchants, who heartily assisted the purpose of the young missionary. He also obtained a letter from the Secretary of State at Washington to the American consul at Canton, where he lived for a year in the factory of some New York merchants. The difficulties and dangers of his position and of those natives whose assistance he needed in the study of the language, were so great that for a while he clothed himself in Chinese dress and adopted Chinese methods of living. After a year, however, his health becoming impaired, he was driven to Macao, a Portuguese possession, but a little later (1809), on his marriage to the daughter of an English merchant residing in Canton, he was able to return there and to accept the offer of a position with the East India Company as a translator of Chinese. This gave him an assured place and income and was of advantage to him in his work of translating the Bible and other books into Chinese.

In 1813, the Rev. William Milne and his wife were sent out by the London Missionary Society as associates to Morrison and proved themselves to be invaluable assistants, but later Milne removed to Malacca, where he founded an Anglo-Saxon College. Morrison continued his work, completing the translation of the New Testament into Chinese and compiling an Anglo-Chinese dictionary which was published by the East India Company at a cost of £15,000. In 1814, seven years after his arrival in China, he baptized Tsai-A-Ko, the first Chinese convert to Christianity, and in 1818 the entire Bible was translated into Chinese, a part of this work being done by Dr. Milne.

In 1824-26 Morrison revisited England and was received with honor by George IV, as well as by the Churches and religious societies of the country. He returned to China in 1826, and died there in 1834, [6]"'After twenty-seven of as labori-

[6] "Rex Christus," p. 34.

ous and fruitful efforts as were ever spent by any missionary that ever penetrated the Celestial Empire."

"Dr. Morrison published more than thirty different works, one of which was his monumental dictionary in six quarto volumes." As has been said, "Any ordinary man would have considered the production of the gigantic English-Chinese dictionary a more than full fifteen years' work. But Morrison had, single-handed, translated most of the Bible; had sent forth tracts and pamphlets; had founded a dispensary, and established a college, besides other duties as translator for the Company, and preaching and teaching every day of his life."

That he was able to do this for a long series of years gives one some idea of the indomitable courage and perseverance of the man, for as Dr. Milne himself said, [7]"to acquire the Chinese is a work for men with bodies of brass, lungs of steel, heads of oak, hands of spring-steel, eyes of eagles, hearts of the apostles, memories of angels, and lives of Methuselah."

With Dr. Milne and Dr. Medhurst, Dr. Morrison formed a Chinese trio, equaling in efficiency and influence the great contemporary trio of Indian missionaries, Carey, Marshman, and Ward.

The earliest American missionaries to China were the Revs. E. C. Bridgman, of the Congregational Church, and David Abeel, of the Reformed Dutch Church, who were sent out by the Amer-

---

[7] "Missionary Enterprise," p. 279.

ican Board with which both of these denominations were then connected (1829).

Bridgman was an editor and writer of great ability. He was the founder of the *"Chinese Repository,"* which continued to be issued for over twenty years with good results. [8]"His great work was that of translation, but he also did his full share of direct missionary work in preaching and distributing religious literature. He was of great assistance in the negotiations which went forward between China and the foreign powers. When the plenipotentiaries of the four great treaty powers—England, France, Russia, and the United States—were conducting their negotiations which resulted in the Tient-sin Treaty of 1858, he was consulted by them and frequently translated official documents for them. In his thirty-two years in China he was more intimately connected with and known by the foreign community at Shanghai and Canton than any other missionary, and by all was highly esteemed."

David Abeel is more particularly noted as the one who first interested the Christian women of England and America in organized missionary work for their own sex. He went to China with Bridgman in 1829 as chaplain for the American Seamen's Friend Society, and in 1831 made a tour to Batavia and other Dutch East India possessions to examine the missionary conditions prevailing there. In 1833 he returned to America

---

8 "Encyclopedia of Missions," Article "Bridgman."

by way of Holland, Switzerland, and England, speaking in behalf of missions and so arousing the Christian women of England by his appeals that, in 1834, they formed the "Society for Promoting Female Education in the East," the pioneer of English women's missionary societies. Much later, through the influence of this English society and the growing needs of the work, the pioneer American society, "The Women's Union Missionary Society," was formed in New York (1861), with Mrs. Thomas C. Doremus for its first president.

In 1842, when the treaty ports in China were first opened, Mr. Abeel immediately repaired to Amoy and founded the Amoy Mission, which a few years later (1857) was transferred by the American Board to the care of the Reformed Church in America, by which it has since been conducted. [9]"This work was begun by Mr. Abeel in a hired house under an overshadowing banyan tree in the island of Kolongsu, in Amoy harbor. By his courtliness, affability, and manly consecration he won the favor of both the literary and official classes, as well as of the common people. His health, never vigorous, soon utterly failed, and returning to the United States, he died there in 1844."

It was Dr. Peter Parker of whom it is said, "he opened China on the point of his lancet," and while it is true that successful medical work was done in China before his time by Morrison and

9 "History of the Amoy Mission," p. 9.

Dr. Colledge of the East India Company, it was Dr. Parker who first began a systematic and continued line of work for the medical treatment of native Chinese. [10]He went to Canton as a missionary of the American Board in 1834 and the next year opened a free Ophthalmic Hospital in that city "to disarm prejudice and spread the gospel." [11]"In twelve short weeks the successful cures from this hospital accomplished more in removing the hitherto impenetrable wall of Chinese prejudice and restrictive policy than could have been accomplished in years by the customary missionary work." Later the hospital was enlarged to include general practice. In 1838 he had four students, one of whom became an expert operator. His labors in ten years were abundant, notwithstanding many obstacles. Beginning with a solitary patient, he personally treated over 53,000 people.

In 1840 wars in China compelled Dr. Parker to return to America. He spent the time in telling of the medical work in China, and as a result some medical missionary societies were organized. While in Edinburgh, in 1841, he was also instrumental in organizing the Edinburgh Medical Missionary Society, whose work has been widespread and successful. He afterwards became United States Commissioner to China, and later returned home, where he died in 1888, at the age of eighty-three. The hospital which he started in Canton

[10] "Opportunities," p. 48. [11] "Pioneer Missionaries," p. 142.

still continues a vigorous work, and as it is the first institution of the kind in heathen lands that had as its twofold aim, first, the alleviation of human suffering, and secondly, the extension of Christianity through the influence obtained by the medical treatment of non-Christians, it is entitled to its claim to be the originator of medical missionary hospitals.

Up to 1842 residence and work in China had been difficult for all foreigners because of the restrictive laws of the Chinese Government, but in 1841 what is called the Opium War broke out, occasioned by an attempt of English and French vessels to smuggle into the country a large quantity of this destructive drug. By this unrighteous war the wicked traffic was fixed upon the Chinese people, but an indirect blessing resulted in the opening of five ports, Canton, Amoy, Fu-chau, Ningpo, and Shanghai, to British residence and trade, which privileges were soon extended to all foreigners. With these fresh opportunities, missionary work became still more active. The American Presbyterians began work in Canton in 1842, followed two years later by the Southern Baptists. Two German missions, the Rhenish and the Basel, entered the Kuang-tung Province in 1847, and the Northern Baptists, the English Presbyterians, the Congregationalists, the Methodist, the Episcopal, and other bodies followed rapidly with new missions and reinforcements.

In 1848 the first Protestant Church edifice ever

erected in China for a distinctively Chinese congregation was built by the Rev. William Pohlman, a missionary of the Reformed Dutch Church, working under the American Board at Amoy. Mr. Pohlman collected the money for this building ($3,000), superintended its erection, and was lost at sea on a voyage to Hong Kong to purchase furnishings for the recently completed structure. The building still stands in constant use as a memorial of the first native Protestant Church gathered in China.

Among the missionaries of this early day, Dr. William Ashmore, of the American Baptists, and Rev. William C. Burns, of the English Presbyterians, are noted for their evangelistic work. Mr. Burns was especially useful as a translator of Christian hymns for the use of native congregations, and of these he prepared and published several collections. He also translated the "Pilgrim's Progress" and other useful additions to Chinese Christian literature. [12]In carrying out his ideas he followed two new departures in missionary work. He lived more among the Chinese than any previous worker had done, dressing as a Chinaman and eating Chinese food, and he took the risk of itinerating widely beyond the stipulated limits of the treaty ports. Burns's life, it has been said, was "more powerful as an influence than as an agency."

The T'ai P'ing Rebellion broke out in China

[12] "Missionary Expansion," p. 149.

in 1850, and was injurious not only to the peace of the country, but to the Christian religion, because its leader, Hung-Hsiu-Chuan, claimed that he was a Messiah like Jesus Christ and incorporated into his declarations some Christian tenets.

The movement, however, soon became fanatical and revolting in its excesses, and finally (1865) it was suppressed by the Government troops led by British and American officers, among whom the most conspicuous was the brave and able English Christian soldier, Charles G. Gordon, "Chinese Gordon," so called because of his eminently successful services in this war as the commander of the Chinese Imperial Army.

During the third period (1860-1895) into which the progress of Chinese missions is sometimes divided, the expansion of missions went on rapidly. By the treaty of Peking (1860), following the close of the so-called "Arrow" war, the liberties and privileges of foreigners were enlarged and religious freedom was permitted to Chinese converts. China also began to see the benefits of Western life and knowledge and to welcome modern education and training.

Among other names of those who came into the work about this time we may mention only those of Griffith John, W. A. P. Martin, J. Hudson Taylor, and James Gilmour, of Mongolia, as being typical of the inauguration or development of certain specific lines of work.

The Rev. Griffith John was a Welshman, who was sent out by the London Missionary Society in 1861, and assigned to pioneer work in the interior of China. He went about seven hundred miles up the Yang-tse River to Han-Kow, the largest commercial center of Middle China, where he established a station, noted as being the pioneer inland mission of the Protestant Church. His labors here were particularly successful and were the entering wedge for the work of a number of other societies.

Dr. W. A. P. Martin, a missionary of the American Presbyterian Board, is noted not only as a missionary educator, but as having obtained a large influence among Chinese scholars. [13]"He went out in 1850, assisted in making the treaty between the United States and China in 1858, and was an authority in China on questions of international law. He was professor in and president of Tung Wen College (1868-1898) and the president of the New Imperial University until 1900, when it was destroyed in the siege of Pekin. In 1902 he was appointed head of the vice-regal University of Wuchong. His influence in directing the rearrangement of higher education in China and in commending Western and Christian education to Chinese scholars has been very marked.

Dr. J. Hudson Taylor has been called "the Loyola of Protestant Missions," and will ever be remembered in the missionary history of China

---

[13] United Editors' Encyclopedia; also, Beach, "Geography and Atlas," p. 300.

as the founder of the China Inland Mission (1866).

[14]"We must devote," as says Dr. Warneck, "a somewhat fuller notice to this mission for this reason, that not merely the strong personality of its founder, but also his Christian and missionary principles have since exercised a great influence upon wide circles and have not inconsiderably altered the carrying on of missions. Two sorts of principles, which concern partly the missionary instruments and partly the missionary task, gave to this China mission its wholly peculiar cast. As to the former, they are the three following: (1) The acceptance of missionaries from all sections of the Church, if only they personally possess the old Scriptural faith. This made the new mission interdenominational. (2) To qualify for missionary service, spiritual preparation is essential, but not an educational training. Missionaries from the universities are welcome, but equally so are such as have had the simplest schooling; it is imperative only that they have Bible knowledge and acquire the Chinese language. Also no difference is made as to sex. Women are as qualified for the service of missions, even for missionary preaching, as are men. And so at least half the missionaries of this society—if married women are included, almost two-thirds—are women, and since its foundation the number of women entering upon missionary serv-

[14] "History of Protestant Missions," pp. 104, 105.

ice has steadily increased. (3) No direct appeal is ever to be made for contributions to the expenses of the missions, nor are the missionaries to reckon upon a fixed salary, but must depend for their maintenance solely upon that which God supplies. In a specific sense, they are to be faith missionaries.

"The second series of principles is virtually determined by the expectation of the approaching second advent of Jesus. They have in view the hastening of His coming by accomplishing the preaching of the gospel as speedily as possible through the whole world (Matt. 24:14). And so witness-bearing is regarded as the essence of the missionary task. Since the matter in hand is not Christianizing, but only that the gospel be heard in the whole world, the missionary commission is limited to evangelization. Planting stations, building up congregations, educational work, extensive literary work, etc., are not absolutely necessary. Itinerant preaching is the chief thing; albeit practical good sense and experience have largely modified this principle, and stations have been organized almost everywhere.

"Again, in order to bring the gospel within the hearing of all nations, the largest possible hosts of evangelists must be sent out. On the basis of these theories, large bands of evangelists were sent out within a short time. Especially when, through the so-called 'Cambridge Seven,' a very storm of enthusiasm for the China Inland Mission was stirred in 1885, the sending out of missionaries increased and that not alone from England, but also from Scandinavia, Germany, America, and Australia. Before 1900 the number of missionaries of this mission was given as 811, of whom 484 were women. However, only seventy-five of the 327 men were ordained. The income in that year was over £50,000 ($245,000). The number of its Chinese communicants scattered through fifteen provinces was about 8,500.

"The Boxer uprising of 1900 smote the work of the China Inland Mission most severely of all the Chinese missions. Almost all of their inland stations had to be abandoned, and of their workers fifty-eight (exclusive of children) were murdered. Since 1901 the work has been taken up with fresh energy and the number of workers has been raised to 898, including 542 women, while the number of communicants has risen to 19,049."

MONGOLIA

Besides China proper, of whose evangelization we have been speaking, there are several dependencies included in the Chinese Empire, of which the most important are Manchuria, Mongolia, Chinese Turkestan, and Thibet. We can refer only to mission work in Mongolia as typified by the experience of James Gilmour, "Gilmour of Mongolia" as he is called. He was a Scotchman, educated at Glasgow and the theological college of Cheshunt, near London, and sailed for China in 1870, commissioned by the London Missionary Society. The field which he attempted almost single-handed to evangelize, and in which only a few scattered traces of earlier Christian missionaries could be found, is one-third as large in area as the United States with a roving population of about 2,500,000. [15]"It is a vast plain about 3,000 feet above the sea level, almost without wood or water, and has as its center and a third of its area the desert of Gobi, or Shamo—'the sand sea.' The very dry air and extreme elevation of this country give a climate so excessively cold that the mercury often remains frozen for several weeks. The winter lasts nine months, and during the short summer there are days of stifling heat usually followed by cold nights. The inhabitants are as a rule nomads, whose chief property is in horses, cattle, sheep and the double-humped or Bactrian camel. There are, however, many villages and towns, and the country abounds in the lamasaries or monasteries of Lamaism, solidly built with brick or stone, adorned with carvings, sculpture, and paintings, well endowed and often having in residence a living Buddha who is worshipped as a divine incarnation."

To this inhospitable and most difficult country Gilmour devoted his life, living in the black tents of the natives, following them from place to place, enduring for weeks and months their squalor and wretchedness, and ministering as a

---

15 "United Editors' Encyclopedia." "Mongolia."

the fact that the indemnity exacted from China as damages, by European and American governments, amounted to no less than 450,000,000 taels, or $333,000,000.

In the reaction however which set in, there is much of hope for China. The adoption of western thought and methods has been hastened by that which was intended to retard them. The century-old methods of education have been largely supplanted by the science and literature of Europe and America. The army and navy, although far from adequate, have been reorganized on European models. Transportation has been revolutionized and, best of all, the advance of Christian missions has been greatly stimulated so that in point both of numbers and of influence, Christianity is far ahead of its position before the Boxer outbreak.

It is however in the apparent success of the political revolution of 1913 that the greatest changes in China are manifested. Aroused by the insufficiency of the ancient methods to protect China from turmoil within or foreign aggression from without, many patriots among whom notably was Sun Yat-sen, worked for the rehabilitation of the Chinese government. Years of planning and preparation preceded the actual outbreak between the Manchu rulers and the progressive elements. At last, early in 1913, the revolutionary spirit blazed forth with irrepressible fury and after a period of disorder of only four months, the

Manchu dynasty, having proved its incompetence to deal with the new problems of old China, passed away, and was replaced by a Republic with a National Assembly, the outline at least of a Constitution, and Sun Yat-sen as the Provisional President, which office he later voluntarily yielded to Yuan Shi-kai. The first election of a permanent president was held, according to the French system, by the National Assembly, in October, 1913, when Yuan Shi-kai was elected as permanent President and Li Yuan-hung as Vice-president. The effect of these changes is already seen in a wonderful quickening of the national consciousness and the opening of innumerable avenues of advancement. The five striped flag of the new Republic, red for China proper, yellow for Manchuria, blue for Mongolia, white for Thibet and black for the Mohammedans, indicates a unity of purpose and power of the leading races to which China has heretofore been a stranger, but over all, though unrepresented in its national ensign, must float the banner of the Christ, if China would realize what is the true source of that uprightness of character and nobility of purpose and purity of faith which after all is the only hope of this great people and which can only be gotten by their willing obedience to the truth as it is in Jesus.

As says the Rev. Dr. F. L. Hawkes Pott, President of the Episcopal Mission University of St. John at Shanghai, and a man who is very close to